Living with Leviathan

Public Spending, Taxes and Economic Performance

Living with Leviathan

Public Spending, Taxes and
Economic Performance

DAVID B. SMITH

The Institute of Economic Affairs

First published in Great Britain in 2006 by
The Institute of Economic Affairs
2 Lord North Street
Westminster
London SW1P 3LB
in association with Profile Books Ltd

The mission of the Institute of Economic Affairs is to improve public
understanding of the fundamental institutions of a free society, by analysing
and expounding the role of markets in solving economic and social problems.

Copyright © The Institute of Economic Affairs 2006

The moral right of the authors has been asserted.

All rights reserved. Without limiting the rights under copyright reserved above,
no part of this publication may be reproduced, stored or introduced into a
retrieval system, or transmitted, in any form or by any means (electronic,
mechanical, photocopying, recording or otherwise), without the prior written
permission of both the copyright owner and the publisher of this book.

A CIP catalogue record for this book is available from the British Library.

ISBN-10: 0 255 36579 9
ISBN-13: 978 0 255 36579 6

Many IEA publications are translated into languages other than English or
are reprinted. Permission to translate or to reprint should be sought from the
Director General at the address above.

Typeset in Stone by MacGuru Ltd
info@macguru.org.uk

Printed and bound in Great Britain by Hobbs the Printers

CONTENTS

THE AUTHOR

David B. Smith studied Economics at Trinity College, Cambridge and the University of Essex in the 1960s. He has since been employed at the Bank of England, the Royal Bank of Scotland, National Westminster Bank, Cambridge Econometrics, the London Business School and the London stockbrokers Williams de Broë. David is currently a Visiting Professor in Business and Economic Forecasting at the University of Derby, chairman of the IEA Shadow Monetary Policy Committee, and a visiting lecturer at the Cardiff University Business School. He was also a member of the Economics Board of the Council for National Academic Awards in the late 1970s and early 1980s. David has written articles on economic forecasting, economics websites, monetary economics and European Monetary Union, as well as on public spending and economic performance. He is perhaps best known for his quarterly macroeconomic model of the international and UK economies, which has existed since the early 1980s, and whose forecasts are now published under the name 'Beacon Economic Forecasting'. He is not related to the Economics Editor of the *Sunday Times*, David H. Smith, with whom he is occasionally confused.

FOREWORD

In this monograph, David Smith illustrates how important it is that politicians detach themselves from the noise and pressures of day-to-day politics and keep in touch with the arguments for economic policies that promote welfare. His reminder is very timely. The views of the three main parties on the level of government spending and taxation are now virtually identical. Yet David Smith shows what could happen if one party were to take a different course, were to be elected to office, and then were to implement new policies.

The evidence presented in this monograph suggests that the optimal level of government spending is probably somewhere between 17 and 30 per cent below its current level in the UK, these amounts representing some 10 to 15 percentage points of national output. If government spending had been kept at the more moderate level experienced in the early 1960s, GDP would almost certainly have risen more quickly and pre-tax incomes might well be double what they are today: post-tax incomes would have more than doubled.

Public sector waste is always inexcusable, but there is little point trying to reduce the size of government through a war on government waste. Waste can be reduced substantially only when the government does less. Indeed, if the UK government had the same level of efficiency as its most efficient OECD counterparts, then the current level of services could probably be provided for £40–80 billion less than their cost today. The positive correlation between the level of waste and the size of the government sector means, however, that a high level of efficiency is unlikely to be achieved unless the scale of government is smaller.

But should we be so obsessed by the economic growth that would come from reduced government spending? What about 'general well-being' – a phrase so beloved by politicians at the moment? If we measure general well-being by what people want, rather than by what politicians think people want, then surely that would improve even more dramatically than national income if the size of government were reduced. People would have more choice in health and education – they would not simply have to put up with what they were given. The poor would have some hope of escaping the mediocre education they are served up on a take-it-or-leave-it basis. Higher post-tax incomes would allow higher savings for old age and illness. Those who chose to do so, perhaps parents with children, could work fewer hours if individuals were not working over two days a week to pay their tax bills.

With rigorous and thorough economic analysis, encompassing both theory and empirical evidence, David Smith shows how damaging politicians' addiction to spending other people's money has been. Even when public spending comes at no cost to its 'beneficiaries' in terms of taxation it seems to damage its recipients. Much public spending for the people of Scotland, Wales, Northern Ireland and northern England is financed by the taxpayers of southern England. But it still harms the economic welfare of those on whom the money is spent. High levels of benefits, relative to the cost of living, price the less skilled out of work, reduce employment and give rise to a socially debilitating dependency culture.

Why do politicians ignore the compelling evidence? Why do they end up systematically destroying the economic welfare of the people they wish to govern? The answer lies in public choice economics. Politicians cannot achieve anything unless they are elected. The interest groups that want more government spending are stronger than those that want lower taxes. The current pattern of government spending creates 'clients' who gain from further expansion. David Smith believes that it is time for politicians to appeal to principles once again. If politicians who wish to cut the size of the state are then elected, they should put in place mechanisms to ensure that those who vote for profligacy bear the cost. One way this can be achieved is by giving more fiscal responsibility to lower tiers of government, but this has to be done in ways that ensure that representation and taxation are clearly linked.

The views expressed in this monograph are, as in all IEA publications, those of the author and not those of the Institute (which has no corporate view), its managing trustees, Academic Advisory Council Members or senior staff.

PHILIP BOOTH

Editorial and Programme Director,
Institute of Economic Affairs
Professor of Insurance and Risk Management,
Sir John Cass Business School, City University
October 2006

SUMMARY

- In the last 90 years the proportion of national income spent by the UK government has increased from around 10 per cent to nearly 50 per cent. This general trend has been followed in most other developed countries, although levels of government spending are much higher in the European Union than in the USA, Australia, Japan and Switzerland.
- The 'optimal' size of the public sector is probably no more than 30–35 per cent of GDP. Government spending at those levels could provide defence, policing, a range of public goods and a basic welfare system.
- If those national governments that lost the greatest amounts of money through waste reduced their levels of waste to that of the most efficient government they could save over one third of the costs of government spending. It does not appear to be possible, however, to cut waste without cutting the size of government. Governments that spend the biggest proportion of national income waste more as a percentage of their spending. Thus a 'war on waste' alone will tend to be ineffective.
- The increase in government spending may explain the chronically poor growth performance of the European Union in recent decades. The performance of the relatively

faster-growing economies, such as the UK, however, would have been much better if government spending had been lower. If government spending, as a proportion of national income, had been held at the level experienced in 1960, econometric evidence suggests that output in the UK would, today, be nearly twice as high as current levels. Total public expenditure would then be higher, albeit as a lower proportion of a much bigger national output.

- Britain has a particularly badly designed tax system. Furthermore, government spending is borne by only part of the population because so many people are in receipt of benefits or 'tax credits'. Marginal tax rates are therefore very high for most working people on moderate incomes or above. After income tax, national insurance contributions and VAT a basic-rate taxpayer will surrender to the state over half of each additional pound that is earned – this is before allowing for excise duties, council tax and travel-to-work costs.
- There are large differences in the levels of taxation and government spending in different regions of the UK. The north-east of England, Scotland, Wales and Northern Ireland have levels of government spending akin to those found in former communist countries. The east and south-east of England have levels of public spending just above 30 per cent – roughly equivalent to the levels found in the lowest-spending OECD countries. After allowing for regional differences in the cost of living, public spending is over 50 per cent higher in Scotland and Northern Ireland than it is in south-east England.
- The high levels of public spending in certain regions of the UK are not reflected in a higher tax take in those regions.

Therefore, they effectively represent transfers from other regions. Even money that is transferred from low-spending to high-spending regions may, however, cause serious economic damage in the recipient region.

- The public choice literature explains why the government sector is so much bigger than the optimal level. Significantly less than half the number of people on the electoral register are employed in the private sector or are self-employed. Parties supporting high tax and redistributive policies become entrenched in this situation – as we can see by examining the policies of all major parties today.

- There is likely to be an increasing government budget deficit in the next few years. Attempts to cut that deficit by raising taxation will fail because of the adverse effects of increased taxes on economic growth.

- Government spending needs to be cut and a flat tax created, possibly with no threshold before individuals start to pay tax – so that all people contribute something in taxation. For public choice reasons, fiscal reform may only be possible after constitutional reform that creates more local autonomy and fiscal responsibility. Regional justice must be restored – arguably there should be *lower* levels of cash public spending in regions where living costs are lower.

TABLES, FIGURES AND BOXES

AUTHOR'S PREFACE

This monograph is concerned with the effects of public spending – and the taxes required to finance it – on a country's economic performance, with special reference to the consequences for the level and growth of national output. This topic is at the heart of the political debate in most countries. It is also, however, one of the most important issues in economics. This is partly because the state is the largest player in modern societies, and often tries to control via regulation economic resources that it does not take in taxes. A more important reason, however, is that the high degree of government intervention in many Western nations poses a threat to personal liberty. In addition, there are grounds for believing that today's welfare states have done more harm than good to their intended beneficiaries at least in part because high social overhead costs have priced low marginal productivity workers out of employment, fostered a dependency culture and broken the ladders of opportunity through which poor people self-improved in the past.

The present predominance of the public sector in Europe has made it easy to overlook how much smaller the state was, even in the early 1960s, let alone before the two world wars. The political debate in most European countries has also ignored the massive differences between the degree of socialisation in similar economies, or between different regions of one country. Thus, general government outlays as a share of national output measured gross of indirect taxes range from around one fifth, or under, in many South-East Asian 'tiger' economies to 56.5 per cent in Sweden. Likewise, the regional analysis presented in Chapter 5 reveals that, within the UK, the share of general government expenditure within the equivalent measure of regional gross domestic product (GDP) ranges from 31.3 per cent in south-east England to 66.2 per cent in Northern Ireland.

Chapters 3 and 4 examine a wide range of evidence dealing with the effects of public expenditure on economic performance, as revealed by macroeconomic model simulations, cross-section and panel data studies and the fiscal stabilisation literature. Chapter 6 investigates whether it is possible to estimate the optimal size of the public sector in practice, before examining why the government spending share frequently seems to have overshot this optimum. Much of the evidence reviewed comes from international sources. The public spending issue is, however, especially topical in Britain now that the Labour government has greatly increased the share of national output absorbed by the state at a time when other countries are paying lip service to the need for fiscal consolidation. The British political context is discussed in Chapter 7. Unfortunately, British politicians have discussed these matters at such a low level of economic literacy since the 1990s that government expenditure has been effectively treated as a painlessly financed 'free good' by all three major parties. This means that the opportunity costs of high spending have been ignored and almost none of the vast body of objective research into the effects of government spending and taxation on economic performance has found its way into the political debate. Chapter 8 draws policy conclusions.

Figure 1 Alternative schematic representations of political ideologies

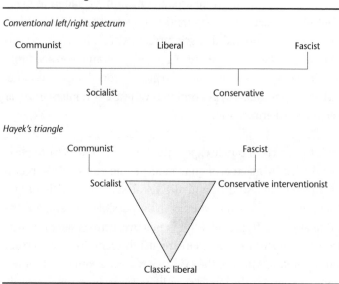

Conventional left/right spectrum

Hayek's triangle

Ideological clarification and Hayek's Triangle

Before proceeding to the main analysis, however, and in an attempt to explain why this monograph is about economics and not inter- or intra-party politics, it seems sensible to first clarify the ideological issues involved using 'Hayek's Triangle'. Figure 1 presents a simple graphical exposition of the analysis set out in the chapter 'Why I am not a Conservative' in Hayek's *Constitution of Liberty*, published in 1960. Here, Hayek made the point that most commentators believe that there is a simple left/right spectrum in politics, whereas, in reality, there is a triangle with classic Gladstonian Liberals at one point, interventionist Bismarckian euro-conservatives at another, and socialists at a third. The extra, second dimension in the triangle corresponds to increasing personal liberty as one moves down the page, a concept absent from the simple linear representation of the left/right spectrum.

Hayek also believed that the difference between classical liberals, such as the authors of the Swiss and US constitutions, with their belief that political legitimacy flowed up from individuals to the state, and conservative interventionists, such as the Roman emperors, Bismarck or the Bourbon monarchs, who believed that all power flowed down from the state, could be as great as that between both groups and overt socialists (see Bastiat, 2001, for a fascinating mid-nineteenth-century French perspective on these issues). Since these political topics are a digression from the purpose of this monograph, they cannot be discussed much further here. The reasons for the apparent internal splits in both Britain's Liberal Democrat and Conservative parties between paternalist-interventionists and libertarians (so-called 'wets' and 'dries' in the 1980s Conservative Party terminology) can, however, be readily comprehended using Hayek's Triangle. David Cameron's current strategy as Conservative leader can also be understood in these terms. He is trying to move his party's perceived image from the allegedly 'nasty' classical liberalism of Lady Thatcher to the claimed 'more caring' socialist/Conservative interventionist zone, although whether concepts such as caring and nasty have any place in a positive applied science such as economics is questionable. Engineers, for example, do not talk about caring and nasty girders, or otherwise engage in psychobabble, because they employ the positivist philosophical approach accepted by all scientists. The marketing brilliance of the Blair project was to promise the electorate that New Labour had moved from the socialist part of the triangle to the classical-liberal part and would maintain Lady Thatcher's low tax policies, although Gordon Brown in the event covertly implemented socialist spending policies, for which New Labour had no electoral mandate. Hayek's *Constitution of Liberty* represents a true classic, in the sense that his words shine as brilliantly today as when they were minted, and his analysis is recommended to those who want to investigate these issues further. Meanwhile, it should be clear that the arguments that follow come from an unashamedly classical liberal or libertarian direction. This means that they are evidence-based as far as is possible and do not support the views of any political party or faction, but rather a set of ideas that have been unduly neglected in the intellectually vacuous British political debate of recent years.

Living with Leviathan

Public Spending, Taxes and Economic Performance

1 PUBLIC SPENDING AND THE SIZE OF THE STATE

This chapter provides a brief introduction. It examines the increased role of the state globally and in Britain since the late nineteenth century, considers the theoretically optimal size of the public sector, raises the question of whether the political process imposes an unduly high rate of time discount, and looks at the issue of government waste.

The increasing role of the public sector

Any attempt to quantify the share of national output absorbed by the state is bedevilled by the measurement difficulties discussed in Chapter 2. The broad trends are, however, sufficiently clear to suggest that the increased role of the state represented one of the main developments of the twentieth century. This can be seen from the statistics for a wide range of nations presented in Table 1 below. The table draws heavily on the famous study of Tanzi and Schuknecht (2000), updated using figures from the annexe to the June 2006 *Economic Outlook* published by the Organisation for Economic Cooperation and Development (OECD). Unfortunately, there are some inconsistencies between the two sources which appear to have arisen from the introduction of new ways of compiling national accounts in recent years, and attention is drawn to the note to Table 1. The combined figures show a rise in

Table 1 **Ratios of public expenditure, including transfers, to money GDP at market prices (%)**

	1870	1913	1920	1937	1960	1980	1990	2005
Australia	18.3	16.5	19.3	14.8	21.1	34.1	35.2	34.9
Austria	10.5	17.0	14.7	20.6	35.7	48.1	51.5	49.6
Belgium	–	13.8	–	21.8	30.3	58.6	52.2	50.1
Canada	–	–	16.7	25.0	28.6	38.8	48.8	39.3
France	12.6	17.0	27.6	29.0	34.6	46.1	49.3	54.4
Germany	10.0	14.8	25.0	34.1	32.4	47.9	44.5	46.8
Ireland	–	–	–	–	28.0	48.9	43.1	34.6
Italy	13.7	17.1	30.1	31.1	30.1	42.1	53.5	48.2
Japan	8.8	8.3	14.8	25.4	17.5	32.0	31.8	36.9
Netherlands	9.1	9.0	13.5	19.0	33.7	55.2	53.1	45.7
NZ	–	–	24.6	25.3	26.9	38.1	49.6	40.6
Norway	5.9	9.3	16.0	11.8	29.9	43.8	54.0	42.9
Spain	–	8.3	9.3	18.4	18.8	32.2	42.6	38.2
Sweden	5.7	10.4	10.9	16.5	31.0	60.1	61.3	56.4
Switzerland	16.5	14.0	17.0	24.1	17.2	32.8	30.0	36.4
UK	9.4	12.7	26.2	30.0	32.2	43.0	42.2	45.1
USA	7.3	7.5	12.1	19.4	27.0	31.4	37.1	36.6
Unweighted average of countries with no missing observations*	10.7	12.4	19.3	23.2	27.9	42.6	44.8	44.0

Sources: Tanzi and Schuknecht (2000); IMF, including *World Economic Outlook*, May 2000 (see especially IMF Table 5.4, p. 172); and *OECD Economic Outlook* (June 2006, Annexe Table 26).

Note: Unfortunately there are some substantial discrepancies between the Tanzi and Schuknecht (T&S) and OECD data for the overlap year of 1990, and the figures should be regarded as illustrative only. The known breaks in 1990, defined as 'OECD–T&S', are: Australia +0.3, Austria +12.9, Belgium –2.1, Canada +2.8, France –0.5, Germany –0.6, Italy +0.1, Ireland +1.5, Japan +0.5, Netherlands –0.6, New Zealand +8.3, Norway –0.9, Sweden +2.2, Switzerland –3.5, UK +2.3 and USA +4.3. These changes appear to have resulted from the adoption of ESA95 national accounting principles after the T&S data were compiled, and might also reflect the problems T&S faced in picking up the expenditure of lower tiers of government in federal systems, among other factors.

* Excludes Austria and New Zealand. The mean break in 1990, as defined above, is +0.3 percentage points.

the government spending ratio for the 'typical' Western economy, from an unweighted average of just under 12.5 per cent in 1913 to 44 per cent in 2005. If government spending is defined widely to include transfer payments, and the GDP concept employed is the somewhat misleading market-price measure, which includes indirect taxes and subsidies as part of national output.

There is an interesting contrast between the increase in the ratios of public spending to GDP in much of 'Old Europe' since 1960, shown by Table 1, with the more moderate rise in the USA. It is also striking how low the spending ratios were 45 years ago in countries such as Sweden, where a large state is now assumed to be an unalterable fact of life. The Swedish experience is unusually significant because of the extent to which the Scandinavian model is now being held out as an exemplar, in Continental Europe and by people close to Gordon Brown. Sweden provides an ambiguous case study, however, because its government spending burden peaked at 72.4 per cent in 1993 and is projected by the OECD to be 55.5 per cent in 2007, representing a decline of 16.9 percentage points. Likewise Sweden's general government tax and non-tax receipts peaked at 64.8 per cent of market-price GDP in 1989 and are expected to be 57.7 per cent next year, or a decline of 7.1 percentage points. Such figures mean that it is indeterminate whether the country's recent economic performance reflects its interventionist approach – as is alleged by its proponents – or the fact that it has rolled back the frontiers of the public sector. In the 'error-correction' framework employed in econometric modelling one would expect economic performance to reflect both the level of government intervention and its rate of change, as well as a multitude of other factors. As a result, it is unclear what lessons can be drawn from the Swedish model, in the absence of a detailed quantitative analysis.

A final comment on Table 1 is what moderate spenders Mussolini and Hitler appear to have been in 1937, compared with their counterparts in today's allegedly free and democratic Europe. This comparison should give rise to libertarian concern, since a citizenry without independent resources cannot stand up to a predatory state, especially when that state also employs the intrusive regulations that were so beloved of fascists and are now such a feature of the contemporary European social model. These issues are discussed further in Chapter 7.

Table 2 below shows an analysis of the ratio of British government spending to GDP, broken down by category and shown at decade intervals. The historical part of Table 2 appeared originally in Smith (1981) and, unlike in Table 1, GDP is expressed 'at factor cost', that is net of indirect taxes and subsidies. Unfortunately, major changes to the national accounts from 1998 onwards made it impossible to update the original version of the table, which used the concept of general government expenditure, beyond the mid-1990s, for reasons that will be discussed in Chapter 2. A set of figures for the total public sector, which also includes public corporations, extending back to 1946, is, however, published regularly by the UK Office for National Statistics (ONS – see Box 1 for details) and these statistics have been used to fill in the figures from 1950 onwards. The fact that 1950 is given on both the old and the new bases gives some idea of the correction factors that have to be applied if the latest data are to be compared with their predecessors. In particular, the new figures for total spending appear to be running some 0.75 per cent higher in 1950 than the older numbers. This is a small discrepancy when compared with the subsequent growth in the share of public expenditure, even if this discrepancy may have varied over the years. The difficulty of

Table 2 **Ratios of main categories of UK public expenditure to money GDP at factor cost at ten-year intervals (%)**

Pre-ESA95 definitions	Government final current expenditure	Grants to persons	Subsidies	Debt interest	Government investment	Total government expenditure
1870	5.2	0.0	0.0	3.5	0.6	9.3
1880	5.6	0.0	0.0	3.1	1.2	9.9
1890	6.2	0.0	0.0	2.4	0.7	9.3
1900	10.0	0.3	0.0	1.8	1.9	14.0
1910	8.8	0.4	0.0	1.9	1.2	12.3
1920	8.7	2.7	2.2	6.1	1.8	21.5
1930	10.5	5.3	0.6	8.4	3.0	27.8
1938	15.1	5.3	0.8	5.7	3.8	30.7
1950	18.9	6.3	4.2	4.8	4.7	38.9
Wartime peaks						
1917	39.0	0.9	0.5	4.3	0.1	44.8
1944	56.1	5.4	2.8	5.0	1.0	70.4
Post-ESA95 figures						
1950	19.5	5.7	4.1	5.4	4.8	39.6
1960	18.9	6.4	2.1	5.1	3.9	36.7
1970	21.2	8.9	2.0	5.1	5.4	42.9
1980	25.2	11.8	2.5	5.9	3.0	48.5
1990	23.4	12.2	1.0	4.2	3.0	43.8
2000	23.8	13.7	0.6	3.2	1.5	42.7
2005	28.0	13.2	0.7	2.4	2.1	46.3

Sources: Feinstein (1972); ONS, *National Income Blue Book* (various dates); ONS, *Economic Trends: Annual Supplement,* 2005 edn; and author's estimates.
Note: The table omits 'Net Current Grants Abroad', which is why the total exceeds the items shown. 'Other Current Grants' have been consolidated with 'Government Final Expenditure' in the ESA95 figures. The figures for 1900 and 1950 are distorted by the Boer War and the Korean War, respectively. The pre-ESA95 data refer to general government, the post-ESA 95 figures to the total public sector.

measuring the tax and spending burdens in practice will subsequently emerge as a major theme of this monograph, together with how easy it is for the concepts employed by theoretical economists to get lost in this statistical fog. In Chapter 2, Table 9 provides a detailed analysis of the effects of recent definitional changes while Table 5 breaks down government spending and receipts on a financial year basis since 1955/56.

One striking thing that stands out from Table 2 is that the GDP costs of the modern welfare state are comparable with those of fighting World War I. This can also be seen from the labour market statistics, where the average mobilisation between 1915 and 1918 of 3.67 million (the peak was 4.43 million in 1918) represented 17.3 per cent of total employment, while the lower of the two official figures for general government employment in 2005, at 5.51 million, represented 17.8 per cent of the employed and self-employed. The absorption of resources on such a scale may explain why the British economy for a period in the 1970s developed many of the symptoms traditionally only associated with periods of wartime finance, such as high inflation, slow growth, large budget deficits and a run-down infrastructure.

The optimal size of the public sector

This monograph is primarily concerned with reviewing the effects of government spending on economic performance, rather than with a detailed analysis of government spending per se, although the latter clearly represents an important topic, which lies at the heart of the political debate. The regional distribution of spending within the UK is examined more thoroughly in Chapter 5, however, because of the light it throws on the consequences of public spending and the apparent lack of justice in the UK tax and benefits systems. One reason for not devoting more space to the institutional details of government spending and the tax system

Box 1 **Where to obtain information on UK government spending and taxes**

Readers interested in examining government spending and taxes in more depth, and in getting other viewpoints, might like to read Davies (1998), which is extremely readable but antedates the increase in spending under New Labour, Warburton (2002), which contains papers from a range of contributors, and Miles et al. (2002), whose introduction, dealing with 'The Economics of Public Spending', provides a concise summary. The Institute for Fiscal Studies publishes detailed surveys on its website, of which Adam and Browne's (2006) account of the UK tax system is a representative example (www.ifs.org.uk – click on 'Publications' and then 'IFS Briefing Notes'). In addition, massive amounts of information are provided in official documents, ranging from the annual *Budget Report*, published in March or April, and the *Pre-Budget Report*, published in the late autumn, to the highly detailed information set out in HM Treasury (2006). Some of this official material contains forecasts as well as historical data and can be downloaded from the Treasury's website (www.hm-treasury. gov.uk). A wider perspective can be found in Joumard et al. (2004), whose paper examines public spending issues across a range of OECD member countries.

is the existence of numerous other good accounts (see Box 1). Indeed, the main problem people encounter in this area is that they can easily become swamped by the amount of information that is available.

It is worth noting that there is little dispute among economists that the state should provide a minimal range of 'public goods',

Box 2 **What is the optimal size of the government sector?**

The social-welfare-maximising share of government can be defined as the share of national output at which the discounted net present value of the marginal social utility derived from the extra government spending is equal to the opportunity cost in terms of the net present value of the forgone economic output, and also personal liberty, arising from the need to pay for it. We would expect the marginal social utility of extra spending to fall as spending increased and the opportunity cost of extra spending to rise. Knowing where this optimum occurs is the 'million-dollar' question of political economy, but it is only in

Figure 2   **The optimal share of government spending in national output**

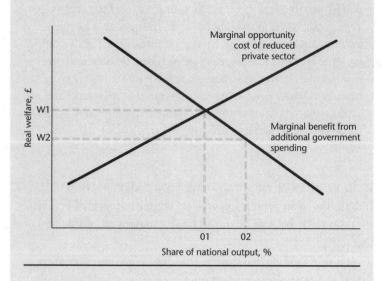

recent years that economists have been able to calculate, even roughly, where this optimal share lies in practice. The research of Tanzi and Schuknecht, discussed in Chapter 6, suggests that general government spending needs to be no higher than 30–35 per cent of the market price measure of GDP to achieve most of the social and political objectives that justify government intervention.

Figure 2 illustrates how extending public spending from its optimal point '01' to '02' reduces the marginal benefit of such spending from 'W1' to 'W2'. The social welfare loss is then the triangular area between the marginal cost and marginal benefit curves above output share 01. The marginal cost and benefit curves have been drawn in linear form for simplicity, but the marginal opportunity cost curve might be expected to be concave with respect to the horizontal axis, while the marginal benefit curve might be expected to be convex. These shapes would then be consistent with the shape of the well-known Laffer curve, for example. Samuelson (1954) provides the classic early analysis of the optimal level of public expenditure.

although there is some debate as to how large this list should be in practice. The conventional examples of public goods tend to include: the defence of property rights; the maintenance of internal law and order; external defence; public health measures, such as those required to counteract epidemics; and, arguably, primary and secondary education. None of these cases is unambiguous and some libertarians would query several of the cited examples. Thus, individuals can do as much to protect their property through basic security measures as the state does, while both education and individual healthcare can be provided by the private sector, and may bring no benefits to society other than the gains to the individuals concerned. It is also possible that, by attempting to do too much, modern Western states have unduly neglected their core functions, as deteriorating law and order and the inadequate resources available to their military on active service seem to testify. A 'nightwatchman' state could probably be provided for around one twentieth of national output, but even the long list of public goods and services can probably be provided using less than one fifth of national output. This means that the public goods argument does not preclude the likelihood that today's far larger government sectors have overshot their social optimum and may have damaged economic and social welfare as a consequence (see Box 2).

Where does the money go?

The economic consequences of different types of government expenditure differ significantly from each other, even if they are funded identically from taxes or borrowing. This suggests that the social-welfare-maximising point defined in Box 2 is a micro-economic concept, which applies to individual spending items, at least as much as it is a macroeconomic criterion applying to government spending as a whole. The international growth litera-ture, as summarised in OECD (2003), for example, suggests that public investment in infrastructure, such as transport links or primary and secondary – but apparently not tertiary – education add to a country's growth potential, and are known as 'productive expenditures', although whether they are best provided for by private enterprise, the state without or with charge, or through

Table 3 **Intended government spending by function, and government receipts in 2006/07**

	(£bn)	(%)	Ratio to GDP at factor cost (%)
Total managed expenditure			
Social protection	151	(27.4)	13.5
Personal social services	26	(4.7)	2.3
Health	96	(17.4)	8.6
Transport	21	(3.8)	1.9
Education	73	(13.2)	6.5
Defence	29	(5.2)	2.6
Debt interest	27	(4.9)	2.4
Industry, agriculture, employment and training	21	(3.8)	1.9
Public order and safety	32	(5.8)	2.9
Housing and environment	19	(3.4)	1.7
Other	57	(10.3)	5.1
Total managed expenditure	**552**	**(100.0)**	**49.3**
Government receipts			
Income tax	144	(27.9)	12.9
National Insurance	90	(17.4)	8.0
Excise duties	40	(7.8)	3.6
Corporation tax	49	(9.5)	4.4
VAT	76	(14.7)	6.8
Business rates	21	(4.1)	1.9
Council tax	22	(4.3)	2.0
Other	74	(14.3)	6.6
Total receipts	**516**	**(100.0)**	**46.1**

Source: HM Treasury, *Budget 2006*, 22 March 2006, Tables C8, C11 and C13, as summarised for Charts 1.1 and 1.2 on p. 13 of *Budget 2006*. There are some discrepancies with Table 6 in this monograph. These largely reflect the treatment of certain tax credits as an expenditure in Table 3 and as a negative tax in Table 6, although there may be other definitional discrepancies.

some hybrid scheme such as Public Private Partnerships (PPPs) remains a subject of debate.

There is also the question of whether the higher taxes required to pay for such investments do more harm to national output than the public investments concerned do good: this issue is examined in Minford and Wang (2006). There is, however, no great need to engage in abstract debates on these issues because the OECD has suggested that only around one fifth of government spending falls into the 'productive' category, and that most other expenditure items are 'non-productive'. Paying means-tested benefits to the working-age population appears to have particularly strong adverse effects on economic growth. Therefore such expenditures are not only 'non-productive' but positively harmful to economic performance, because of their impact on the supply of labour: modern research suggests that the supply of labour is very elastic with respect to the post-tax returns from recorded work compared with living off benefits or working in the underground economy. These important microeconomic distinctions need to be borne in mind later on when it is not always clear which definition of government spending is being employed in a particular study.

Instant versus deferred gratification

In many senses, the real debate over public spending is, arguably, about the extent to which society values instant gratification compared with the deferred benefits (in the form of increased living standards, better life chances and lower structural unemployment) that would result from a smaller government. Politicians are notoriously short-sighted, but especially so when an election is looming. This contrasts with private citizens, who appear to be concerned not just with their living standards over their lifetimes, but the welfare of future generations as well. Many grandparents, for example, devote large amounts of time, and often provide substantial financial support, to their grand-children. As a result, one of the deep-seated forms of damage caused by a large state is the imposition of an excessively high rate of time discount on society at large. A classic illustration of this was Gordon Brown's raiding of private pension funds in order to spend more on public consumption. A particular aspect of this proclivity is that large states tend to smother the future in order to mollycoddle currently powerful vested interest groups, whose roots lie in their past achievements. One example is that industries and social groups that are now ossified, but still politically influen-tial, capture the legislative process (see Bastiat, 2001, but also the public choice literature) and get the government to stop the clock and stifle potential competitors at birth. The fortune expended on supporting agriculture by the EU is a well-known example of this process. There are numerous others, however, especially in Conti-nental Europe and pre-Thatcher Britain. It might even be argued that the socialised provision of medicine and education in Britain has now taken on the characteristics of obsolescent industrial lobbies, whose main aims are to maximise the socialised provi-sion of such services and to block competition from more nimble private providers, rather than the maximisation of the welfare of society.

Unfortunately, there are no political lobbies on behalf of the forgone output and social progress that would have been created by a Hayekian 'discovery process' in a less politicised system of health and education provision. This is because, under an inter-ventionist system, those opportunities for new ways of providing health, education and so on are lost and therefore interest groups representing potential providers can never emerge. One of the noticeable effects of the welfare state is to generate intergenerational transfers from the young and the unborn towards the old,[1] who act as a powerful voting lobby, even if they no longer contribute to the output of society. It is hard to see the social justice in a system under which the generation that sets up an unaffordable welfare state writes blank cheques on the pockets of its children and grandchildren, and hence effectively cannibalises its young. Members of the 'insecure, pressured, over-taxed and debt-ridden' 'iPod' generation of young citizens, who are now starting to feel hard done by, can confirm their suspicions by reading Bosanquet and Gibbs (2005).

Means-tested welfare benefits also tend to transfer resources from people who can defer gratification – such as savers, studiers, investors and the ambitious – and place them in the hands of people who are, on average, more likely to blow everything in the search for instant gratification. This transfer of resources, together with the Chancellor's raid on pension funds, may help explain why Britain's household savings ratio fell from just over 9.5 per cent in 1996 to 4.9 per cent in 2005. To an economist, such penalisation of 'virtue' and subsidisation of 'vice' should have the effect of decreasing the supply of the former and increasing the supply of the latter, provided that the elasticity of supply is greater than zero. These issues were examined from a conceptual perspective using the relatively new approach of behavioural economics by Beaulier and Caplan (2002).

There is also a growing body of quantitative research into the effects of the welfare system on creating dependency, all of

---

[1] This happens through pay-as-you-go pension systems, whereby the taxes of the young are used to pay the pensions of the old and those approaching retirement are promised pensions that will be financed by the taxes of those who cannot vote and may not even be born: see Booth (1998, 1999) for a discussion of the iniquity and inequity of this.

which suggests that the elasticity of supply of welfare claimants is reasonably high, and certainly well above zero. One example is the research carried out by Heitger (2002) into the effects of the tax burden and other labour market interventions on unemployment. Heitger found that a high tax burden had a particularly powerful adverse impact on long-term unemployment, and could explain why there were far higher jobless rates in Continental Europe than in the USA. Another example is the work of Looney (2005), who examined the effects of US welfare reform on single mothers' welfare use and employment in the 1990s, while Matthews et al. (2006) were able to make considerable progress in explaining the incidence of drunken violence in England and Wales, using a panel data approach. A personal view is that this sort of objective quantitative research badly needs to be given more weight in the wider debate over the social and moral effects of welfare dependency (Bartholomew, 2004), which often appears to generate either incandescent rage or mawkish sentimentality.

The waste issue

It has been implicitly assumed until now that all government expenditure generates at least some utility to society at large, even if this does start diminishing beyond a certain point. Like the grey socks that arrive from Aunt Mabel every Christmas, the benefits of state-provided goods and services may be lower than one might hope for because state producers (like Aunt Mabel) have no understanding of the detailed tastes and preferences of the recipients of their goods and services. There is, however, an alternative view that public spending not only provides little benefit at the margin but that, even worse, the government makes highly inefficient use of the productive inputs that it employs and simply wastes many of the resources that it has expropriated from the private sector. It is often argued that this is because government employees do not experience the commercial disciplines that force private sector producers to eliminate the misuse of resources.

The waste hypothesis opens up the possibility that the output of government services can be increased, or taxes reduced, simply by improving the efficiency with which government services are provided. This argument has been put most forcibly in the Taxpayers' Alliance's annual *Bumper Book of Government Waste* (www.taxpayersalliance.com), which seems to have stimulated both the government's Gershon review and the Conservatives' James report into the subject before the 2005 election. In addition to the IEA's own work, the think tanks Reform, Politeia and the Centre for Policy Studies have all published numerous detailed reports looking at the waste issue and have recently been joined at a pan-European level by the relatively new think tank Open Europe. As a result, there is now a substantial literature available to those who wish to investigate these issues further (the websites are: www.reform.co.uk, www.politeia.co.uk, www.cps.org.uk and www.openeurope.org.uk).

Much of this think-tank research is of high quality, looks at the detailed institutional issues involved (see Darwell, 2005, on reforming Whitehall, for example) and is concerned with how reforms can be implemented in practice.

An alternative approach is to compute public sector performance and efficiency indicators for a wide range of countries, and then measure the input and output efficiency of the public sectors concerned using complex econometric techniques. The results of one such investigation, which employed data for 23 developed countries, were published by Alfonso et al. (2003). Their study found significant differences in public sector efficiency across countries, with Japan, Switzerland, Australia, the USA and Luxembourg showing the best values for overall efficiency, and the Eurozone economies often coming out badly (France, Portugal, Italy and Greece occupying the bottom four out of the 23 places in descending order). Britain came sixteenth in the same rankings. The authors also found that countries where the state absorbed a smaller share of national output were significantly more efficient than 'big government' countries, and that the latter could on average save 35 per cent of their costs if they were to catch up with the most efficient countries. As far as the UK is concerned the overall efficiency shortfall in 2000 seems to have been around 16 per cent, although efficiency may have deteriorated subsequently because of the abandon with which resources have been thrown at the public services. The 16 per cent figure implies that the same government services could have been delivered for some £43.5 billion less, if this proportion is applied to 2005/06 general government current expenditure, and £80 billion less if total general government expenditure excluding debt interest, depreciation and net current grants overseas in 2005/06 is used as the base.

From a conceptual viewpoint, the effect of waste can be regarded as shifting inwards the marginal benefit curve from government spending in Figure 2 and also making it slope more steeply downwards, if waste grows with expenditure. It can easily be seen by anyone who is prepared to draw the 'waste-corrected' marginal benefit curve on Figure 2 how waste reduces welfare and lowers the optimal share of government spending in national output.

2 MEASUREMENT PROBLEMS, OLD AND NEW

This chapter examines the conceptual and practical problems involved in quantifying the tax and spending burdens. These measurement concerns are important, and widely misunderstood, issues in the political debate on the size and role of the state. Readers mainly interested in the economic aspects might, however, want to proceed directly to Chapter 3.

Why democracies need reliable figures on government activities

There is a strong need for well-documented and internally consistent figures for public sector activity, and making such data available to citizens should surely be one of the main concerns of official bodies, such as Britain's Office for National Statistics (ONS), in an open democracy. Unfortunately, it is difficult to measure the scale of government activity and how it has changed in Britain with any precision, despite the importance of this issue to democratic accountability. Indeed, it is hard for the outside observer to disentangle the effects of the following: the genuine conceptual and practical problems involved; the institutional failure of the ONS to deliver better figures because of its technical and organisational limitations; and the provision of disinformation by politicians and their representatives. Some measurement difficulties have inevitably arisen because of the changing ways in which governments have organised the delivery of public services over the years. The implementation of the new European Standard Accounts (known as ESA95), however, which happened in a series of stages from 1998 onwards in Britain, also represented a major break with previous data conventions, something that was true for many countries, not just Britain (see note to Table 1). More generally, there are two main reasons why competing measures of the public spending and tax burdens may not be consistent with each other.

How do we define the 'public sector'?

The first is that definitions of the public sector can vary widely, particularly once allowance is made for quasi-government bodies and public corporations. It used to be possible to limit these problems by employing the concept of 'general government', which consists of central government plus local authorities. This concept is widely used for international comparisons, because of the confusion that could otherwise arise from countries with federal systems. It also helps minimise the breaks associated with UK privatisation programmes, which took industries, such as gas, electricity and water supply, out of public corporations and into the private sector. Unfortunately, the distinction between general government and other sectors of the economy has become rather blurred over the years. One reason is that important publicly funded activities – such as NHS trusts – were initially defined as public corporations after they first appeared in 1991 and were only reintegrated back into the general government sector recently. Another reason is that other important state-funded activities and

> **Box 3 Why gross domestic product at factor cost is the least bad measure of national output**
>
> There was a consensus throughout the early post-war period that it was best to measure GDP at factor cost when trying to measure the tax and spending burdens for four main reasons: first, that GDP at factor cost provided a more accurate measure of the national output available to support public consumption; second, that public expenditure paid almost no indirect tax and that a more accurate measure of the spending burden can be achieved if factor cost GDP was used as the divisor; third, that more complex and conceptually superior calculations, which applied 'demand weights' to the individual spending components, produced results very close to the simple factor cost calculation; and finally, that the alternative market-price measure of GDP would rise if there were a move from direct to indirect taxation, even if nothing else had changed. The official decision to switch from the factor cost to the market-price measure of GDP seems to have been implemented in the mid-1970s to massage down the tax and spending ratios, at a time when the public finances appeared to be out of control. Margaret Thatcher's switch from direct to indirect taxes in her first 1979 Budget also made her claim to be a tight-fisted guardian of the public purse look more plausible than it deserved to be, while the rises in excise duties in the early part of Gordon Brown's period as Chancellor has had the same effect.

their employees – such as universities, colleges of further education and 'opted-out' schools – are now allocated to the new ESA95 category of Non Profit Institutions Serving Households (NPISH), which is a hybrid split roughly 80 to 20 per cent between government-funded activities and bodies such as private sector charities (although the latter also receive significant financial support from the government nowadays). The costs to the government of buying in services from the NPISH sector now appear as 'Other Current Grants by General Government', and amounted to just over £33 billion in fiscal 2005/06, or just over 3 per cent of factor cost GDP.

A third change, introduced with ESA95, is that the EU is now treated as a separate fourth arm of government, alongside central government, local authorities and public corporations. This means that taxes paid directly to the EU are no longer included in the UK tax figures, despite the fact that they accounted for £4.25 billion, or not quite 0.5 per cent of GDP, in 2005/06. A final issue is the treatment of tax credits as a negative tax, rather than as the social security benefits that they closely resemble. This again reduces the tax and spending burdens by just under 0.5 per cent of GDP.

How do we define national output?

The second major problem involved in attempts to measure the government spending and tax burdens concerns the precise definition of national output with which public expenditure and tax revenues are to be compared. There are at least three separate ways of measuring GDP, and the chosen option can make a noticeable difference to the ratios concerned. GDP at market prices is reported gross of indirect taxes and subsidies, and overstates national output as a result. Even so, it is the officially preferred measure and is the concept most widely employed for international comparisons, such as in Table 1, because many

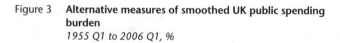

Figure 3   **Alternative measures of smoothed UK public spending burden**
1955 Q1 to 2006 Q1, %

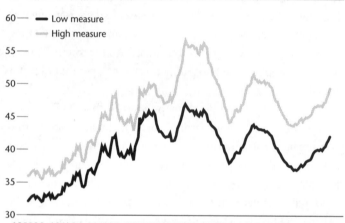

Note: High measure = ratio of total general government spending to non-oil GDP at factor cost; low measure = ratio of total government spending to GDP at market prices.

overseas countries can produce only market-price estimates. The different levels of overall taxation, however, and the varying mixtures between direct and indirect taxes, mean that market-price measures can distort the relative rankings of the economies concerned, and may understate the tax and spending burdens in countries with a high VAT (e.g. European nations compared with the USA). The alternative measure of GDP at factor cost excludes all indirect taxes and subsidies, and is arguably the best measure of national output for both internal purposes and international comparisons. The factor cost measure has, however, been given less prominence by Britain's official statisticians since ESA95 than

Figure 4   **Alternative measures of smoothed UK tax burden**
1955 Q1 to 2006 Q1, %

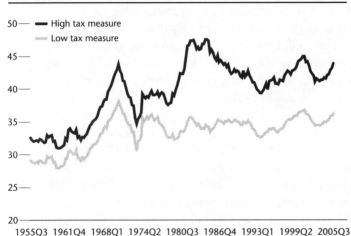

Note: High Tax Measure = ratio of non-oil, EU and oil taxes to non-oil GDP at factor cost; Low Tax Measure = ratio of non-oil taxes to GDP at market prices.

the hybrid GDP at basic prices. This excludes most, but not all, indirect taxes and is sometimes referred to as Gross Value Added (GVA) by the ONS.

General government expenditure measured on a national accounts basis and by economic category

The problems involved in quantifying and tracking the size of the public sector mean that there is no unambiguously correct way to approach the issue. Thus, the demands of the EU for internationally comparable data for legal and administrative purposes

Box 4 **The effects of different GDP concepts on the main tax and spending ratios**

The measure of national output used as an indicator of the burden of public spending and taxes is not just a trivial accounting point (see Table 4 below and Figures 3 and 4). In fiscal 2005/06, for example, the market price measure of national output totalled £1,239 billion, the basic price measure amounted to £1,100 billion, and factor cost GDP was £1,086 billion. This means that the topside market-price variable was some £154 billion (14.1 per cent) higher than the lowest factor cost measure, and that the share of total general government expenditure in money GDP was 41.9 per cent in 2005/06 if the market price measure is used, and 47.8 per cent if the arguably superior factor cost measure is employed instead. This represents a massive difference of 5.9 percentage points. Likewise, the share of non-oil taxes in GDP was 36.5 per cent using the market-price measure, and 41.7 per cent using factor cost – representing a difference of 5.2 percentage points. The latter figure represents the equivalent of 2.75 weeks in the calculation of the much-publicised 'tax-freedom day', when the average citizen ceases to work for the state and starts working for himself (see Smith, 2002). In addition, all these ratios would be noticeably higher if North Sea oil production, which was £21.1 billion in fiscal year 2005/06, is deducted from GDP.

are quite distinct from the needs of econometric modellers for long runs of consistently defined seasonally adjusted quarterly data. The 'least bad' buy for many economic purposes, however, appears to be to employ measures of general government

Table 4 **Alternative measures of the shares of government spending and taxes in UK national output in fiscal year 2005/06**

	Value (£bn)	Share of GGE in GDP (%)	Share of total TNIC in GDP (%)	Share of non-oil TNIC in GDP (%)
General government expenditure (GGE)	519.1			
Total taxes and National Insurance contributions (TNIC)	462.5			
Non-oil taxes & NICs*	452.8			
GDP at current market prices	1,239.3	41.9	37.3	36.5
GDP at basic prices	1,099.9	47.2	42.0	41.2
GDP at factor cost	1,085.7	47.8	42.6	41.7
Non-oil GDP at current market prices	1,218.2	42.6	38.0	37.2
Non-oil GDP at basic prices	1,078.8	48.1	42.9	42.0
Non-oil GDP at factor cost	1,064.6	48.8	43.4	42.5

Sources include ONS, *Financial Statistics*, August 2006 (Table 2.3C); ONS, *UK Output, Income and Expenditure First Release*, 25 August 2006; author's calculations. The market-price spending ratio differs from the OECD one shown in Table 1 because of timing effects (the OECD estimate is for calendar, not fiscal, years), but it is not clear why they differ otherwise. The OECD does, however, rework its figures on to a standard international basis.

* Includes taxes paid directly to the European Union. These totalled £4.2 billion in 2005/06.

expenditure compiled by sub-sector and economic categories on a national accounts basis. Such measures appear to make the most economic sense, which is why they are widely employed in macroeconomic models, even if they do not correspond to any of the 'control totals' employed by HM Treasury. For Table 5, we have shown figures at five-yearly intervals up to 1995/96, but annually from 1996/97 onwards. This allows a comparison

Table 5 Ratios of UK general government expenditure and taxes to money GDP at factor cost for selected benchmark financial years (%)

Financial years	General government final expenditure	Current grants to persons	Subsidies	Debt interest	General government investment	'Other' current grants government	Total general government expenditure	Non-oil taxes	Other government revenues	Total government receipts
'Spot' years										
1955/56	19.4	5.5	2.1	4.6	4.7	0.2	36.5	32.9	4.1	37.0
1963/64	18.6	7.2	2.0	4.4	4.7	0.4	39.8	32.8	3.9	36.7
1965/66	19.4	7.7	1.7	4.3	5.0	0.5	41.3	35.1	4.7	39.8
1970/71	20.7	8.6	2.0	4.4	5.7	0.6	45.0	41.8	5.5	47.3
1975/76	24.1	9.7	3.3	4.6	5.4	0.8	49.7	39.4	5.6	45.5
1980/81	24.7	12.0	2.5	5.6	3.0	0.8	49.9	38.9	5.8	47.0
1985/86	23.7	14.4	1.6	5.8	2.6	0.9	50.0	39.7	5.0	48.3
1990/91	22.7	12.4	1.0	4.1	2.6	0.8	45.3	40.9	3.5	45.0
1995/96	22.4	15.4	0.9	4.2	2.4	1.6	48.5	40.4	3.0	43.8
Annual data										
1996/97	21.6	14.8	0.8	4.1	1.6	1.9	46.3	39.5	2.9	42.9
1997/98	21.6	14.1	0.8	4.1	1.5	1.9	44.7	42.3	2.7	44.4
1998/99	20.8	13.9	0.6	3.9	1.5	2.0	43.3	41.5	2.6	44.5
1999/00	21.2	14.9	0.5	3.2	1.3	2.0	42.7	42.5	2.4	45.2
2000/01	21.8	13.7	0.5	3.2	1.4	2.0	43.3	43.1	2.3	46.0
2001/02	22.3	14.1	0.6	2.6	1.6	2.2	43.9	41.4	2.4	44.5
2002/03	23.3	13.4	0.6	2.3	1.7	2.2	44.7	39.8	2.4	42.7

2003/04	24.1	13.5	0.7	2.3	1.8	2.8	46.1	40.5	2.2	43.1
2004/05	24.4	13.6	0.7	2.4	2.1	3.1	47.0	40.7	2.1	43.3
2005/06	25 1	13.2	0.6	2.4	2.3	3.1	47.8	41.3	2.1	44.3
*HM Treasury forecasts**										
2005/06	25.4	13.4	0.6	2.5	2.3	3.6	48.6	42.0	2.1	45.0
2006/07	25.6	13.2	0.6	2.4	2.5	3.7	49.0	42.6	2.1	45.6
2007/08	25.6	12.9	0.6	2.4	2.6	3.9	48.9	43.0	2.1	46.0

Source: UK National Statistics, including unpublished data from the NS data bank. The table omits a number of spending components, which is why the total exceeds the items shown. Total government receipts also include North Sea oil revenues, which is again why the total exceeds the items shown. Other government revenues covers all non-oil, non-tax receipts.

* Forecasts are derived from HM Treasury, *Budget 2006*, 22 March 2006, Tables C3 and C23. The 2005/06 outcomes are consistent with the August 2006 ONS Financial Statistics (Table 2.3C) and the 25 August ONS GDP news release.

with the last year the Conservatives were in office (1996/97) and shows the initial tight control of public spending in the early years of New Labour's period in power, followed by the less parsimonious policies engaged in more recently. The table also includes the implied HM Treasury forecasts for these items set out in the March 2006 *Budget Report*, although the accuracy of such projections is, of course, debatable. In particular, there appear to be some noticeable discrepancies between the Budget's estimated outcomes for 2005/06 and the latest official estimates of the numbers concerned.

It is also worth bearing in mind that the business cycle can have a substantial effect on the ratio of public sector activity to national output – because government spending and tax receipts both vary with the output gap, while the cyclical swings in GDP can become an independent source of fluctuations in the ratio. The smoother course of national output since the Bank of England was granted operational independence in May 1997 means, however, that the recent cyclical swings in the tax and spending ratios have been smaller than they would have been in many earlier periods. There is a widespread literature on how to estimate cyclically corrected measures of the fiscal deficit, and such calculations both underlie the Chancellor's 'golden rule' – that the current budget should be balanced over the business cycle – and are published regularly for a wide range of countries in the twice-yearly OECD *Economic Outlook* (Annexe Table 28 in the June 2006 edition). The problem with all such calculations, however, is that one has to both estimate potential output – something on which the Bank of England and HM Treasury often have divergent views – and also arbitrarily specify which particular components of GDP would have been different if the economy had been on trend.

This is because the 'tax richness' of the different components of GDP can differ substantially, with household consumption being particularly tax rich, but with government spending, exports and capital formation generating little or no tax revenue. There is also the implicit Keynesian assumption underlying such studies that 100 per cent of the shocks that affect national output come from aggregate demand rather than the supply side. This is not borne out by time series analyses, which typically find that permanent supply shocks to national output are at least as frequent and large as transitory demand shocks. As a result, the view of many macroeconomic modellers appears to be that calculations of the cyclically adjusted fiscal position are of only limited validity, even if politicians were not prone to bend the definitions employed to their own advantage.

GDP includes public spending

A further point when attempting to measure the tax and spending burdens is that GDP on any measure is defined to include public current and capital expenditure, and also consumption financed out of welfare benefits (see Figure 7 in Chapter 4). It can be argued that the state cannot fund itself, and that a more relevant measure of the tax and spending burdens is their ratio to the non-socialised element of national output. This was some 51.25 per cent of the factor cost measure of UK non-oil GDP in 2005/06, for example. Put this way, the state and its beneficiaries are now spending in total 95.25p for every pound spent in the private sector and extracting 83p in non-oil taxes.

This is a highly controversial and unconventional way to estimate the public spending and tax burdens. Essentially, the

Box 5 Where to obtain data on UK government spending

It is possible to obtain financial year totals and the latest quarter's figures for general government transactions by economic category and sub-sector from the ONS publication *Financial Statistics*. A set of forecasts appears regularly in the HM Treasury spring *Budget Report* and the *Pre-Budget Report*, published in the late autumn. The figures for the total public sector, used in Table 2, are available on a quarterly basis back to 1946 in the ONS publication *Economic Trends: Annual Supplement* and can be updated using the monthly edition of the ONS's *Economic Trends*. Unfortunately, the ONS has reduced the information that it used to provide in recent years. Thus, it is no longer possible to obtain a set of seasonally adjusted quarterly figures for government expenditure and receipts by sub-sector and economic category. This is a major nuisance when attempting to project the public accounts partway through the year, because of the seasonal volatility in the data (see Figures 5 and 6). In addition, general government current expenditure and fixed capital formation are not defined consistently in the national and public sector accounts, a pitfall that came in with ESA95. Fortunately, the ONS are still publishing unadjusted figures for general government expenditure and receipts by sub-sector and economic category back to 1946 Q1 in Excel form on their website (www.ons.gov). These statistics are the source for the historical data supplied in Table 5. Table 5 also includes the implied HM Treasury forecasts for these items set out in the March 2006 *Budget Report*. This document provides cash projections for the individual expenditure and receipt items and these have been combined with the HM Treasury figure for market-price GDP given in *Budget 2006*. The Treasury's implied figures for factor cost GDP can then be calculated by subtracting the 'taxes on production and imports', and adding back the subsidies.

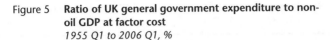

Figure 5 **Ratio of UK general government expenditure to non-oil GDP at factor cost**
1955 Q1 to 2006 Q1, %

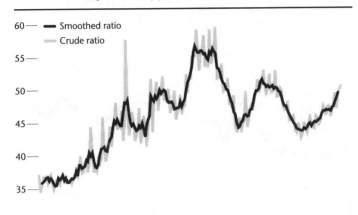

Note: Smoothed ratio is centred four-quarter moving average; crude ratio uses ONS non-seasonally adjusted data for the quarter concerned.

argument is that, if a taxpayer carries one bureaucrat (or welfare recipient) on his or her back, the ratio is one to one, not one to 'one plus one', and that if the taxpayer carries two bureaucrats, the ratio is two to one, not two over three, and so on. This may explain why the tax burden feels more onerous to private sector taxpayers than is shown by the official figures. It also suggests that expressing fiscal balances as a share of total GDP can give a misleading indication of the fiscal responsibility of the government concerned. No sector of the economy can absorb its own debt, and funding a budget deficit becomes progressively more difficult as the share of the private sector in total GDP declines. For example,

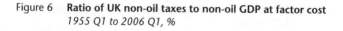

Figure 6   **Ratio of UK non-oil taxes to non-oil GDP at factor cost**
1955 Q1 to 2006 Q1, %

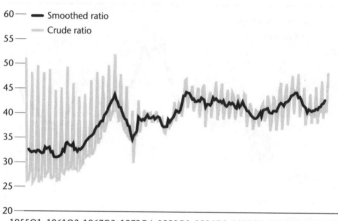

Note: Smoothed ratio is centred four-quarter moving average; crude ratio uses ONS non-seasonally adjusted data for the quarter concerned.

the OECD's projected 2006 US fiscal deficit of 3.6 per cent of total GDP falls 0.6 percentage points below its British equivalent of 3.4 per cent, once allowance is also made for the larger share of the US private sector that is available to finance it (Table 6). Public choice theory suggests that official data is produced by bureaucrats and politicians in order to further their own interests, and not those of the citizenry as a whole. The subconscious intellectual blinkers imposed by dependency on the taxpayer may explain why few people question whether total GDP at market prices is the most appropriate scaling factor for measuring the tax and spending burdens.

Table 6 **Ratios of general government financial balances to money GDP at market prices and non-socialised GDP at market prices (%)**

	Ratio of surplus (+) or deficit (−) to nominal GDP at market prices (%)	Ratio of surplus (+) or deficit (−) to private sector GDP at market prices (%)	Ratio of non-socialised economy to nominal GDP at market prices (%)
Australia	0.9	1.4	65.2
Canada	2.2	3.6	61.1
France	−2.9	−6.4	45.5
Germany	−3.1	−5.8	53.9
Hungary	−5.8	−11.4	50.7
Ireland	−0.3	−0.5	65.2
Italy	−4.2	−8.0	52.2
Japan	−5.2	−8.2	63.3
Korea	2.7	3.3	71.8
Sweden	1.7	3.9	43.3
Switzerland	−0.2	−0.3	63.9
United Kingdom	−3.4	−6.3	54.4
United States	−3.6	−5.7	63.4
Eurozone	−2.3	−4.4	52.7
Total OECD	−2.6	−4.4	59.4

Source: OECD, *Economic Outlook*, vol. 2006/1, no. 79, June 2006, Annexe Tables 25 and 27. Non-socialised GDP is defined as 100 per cent *minus* the share of general government total outlays in GDP, from Table 25. This calculation can be carried out for more countries than those shown here, or using general government receipts from the OECD's Table 26 to define the non-socialised sector. All figures are OECD forecasts for 2006.

Measuring government employment

Private sector employers have to keep meticulous records of their employees. It may come as a surprise, therefore, that the government that imposed these requirements had only a vague idea of the number of people on its own payroll until recently, and that far more people said in answer to surveys that they worked for the public sector than the government stated that it employed. The

Table 7 Alternative estimates of people employed in the public sector

| Mid-years | Data from Administrative Records (000s) | | | | | % of total employment | | | Proportion of employees in trade unions | |
	Central government	Local authorities	General government	Public corporation	Total public sector	Labour Force Survey estimate of total public sector	Administrative measure	Labour Force Survey measure	Public sector	Private sector
1995	2,185	2,759	4,944	424	5,368	6,126	20.8	23.6	61.5	21.6
1996	2,147	2,734	4,881	387	5,268	6,232	20.2	23.8	61.1	20.9
1997	2,107	2,728	4,835	339	5,174	6,046	19.5	22.7	60.9	19.9
1998	2,110	2,710	4,820	342	5,163	6,037	19.3	22.4	61.0	19.5
1999	2,114	2,741	4,855	352	5,207	6,166	19.2	22.6	59.9	19.3
2000	2,153	2,776	4,929	359	5,288	6,282	19.2	22.7	60.2	18.8
2001	2,230	2,777	5,007	371	5,378	6,372	19.4	22.9	59.3	18.6
2002	2,322	2,794	5,116	369	5,485	6,500	19.7	23.2	59.7	18.2
2003	2,432	2,837	5,269	372	5,641	6,616	20.0	23.4	59.1	18.2
2004	2,504	2,891	5,395	361	5,756	6,896	20.3	24.2	58.8	17.2
2005	2,559	2,928	5,487	363	5,850	7,007	20.4	24.3	58.6	17.2
2006*	2,557	2,948	5,505	345	5,859	7,145	20.3	24.8	n/a	n/a

Source: Hicks et al. (2005), Tables 3.1, 4.1 and 4.9, updated using ONS, Public Sector Employment First Release, 30 June 2006, and Grainger (2006), Table 4, for trade union membership.
* Q1 or winter 2005/06.

absence of reliable figures for public sector employment made it difficult to know what was happening to the private sector's demand for labour, or government productivity, and allowed all sorts of ill-founded and politically motivated claims and counter-claims to be bandied about. Fortunately, the ONS have, somewhat belatedly, attempted to reconcile and explain the various sources of public sector employment data (see Hicks et al., 2005) and are now publishing non-seasonally adjusted quarterly figures for government employment with a reasonably short delay.

One source of uncertainty with respect to government employ-ment concerns the fact that administrative records showed that 5,859,000 people worked in the public sector in early 2006, of whom 5,505,000 were in general government with the remainder working in public corporations, while the Labour Force Survey (LFS) at broadly the same date said that 7,145,000 people claimed to be working for the government. The discrepancy of over 1.25 million people partly reflects the fact that people who work for Non Profit Institutions Serving Households, such as universities, or people working for subcontractors, such as agency nurses, or those classified as self-employed, such as general practitioners, are likely to regard themselves as being paid out of the public purse, even if that is not the way the data are defined in the national accounts.

From the taxpayer's viewpoint, of course, it makes little differ-ence whether people paid by the state are on or off the formal records of government employment. It is also possible that even the 7,145,000 figure understates the workforce supported by the taxpayer, because some indirectly funded workers would know that they were not classified as belonging to the public sector. In addition, there are numerous private sector consultants (including many economists) working on government projects, who are only a paper transaction away from being government employees (Heath, 2006b, looks at this 'grey zone' in more detail). The costs involved in hiring the services of such people do appear as a procurement item in general government current expenditure, however, so the total spending figures are correct. Since Labour assumed office in 1997, the administrative measure of public sector employment has increased by 685,000 (13.2 per cent) while the Labour Force Survey measure has increased by 708,000 (13.7 per cent).

The narrower administrative measure of general government employment can be pushed back to the early 1960s by chain-linking on earlier official estimates and adjusting for the defini-tional breaks observed over the years. People who worry about Britain having 'too few producers', to quote from the title of the pioneering study by Bacon and Eltis (1976), would be uncomfort-able with the following facts: 8 million people worked in manufac-turing in 1964 compared with 3.5 million in general government; by 1997 there were under 4.25 million manufacturers and more than 4.5 million on the public payroll; and by April 2006 the number of manufacturing employees was just above 3 million, with 1.8 general government employees, on the administrative measure, for each one in manufacturing. The most noticeable change in the workforce since the early 1960s, however, has been the rise in the 'other' private sector from under 12.75 million employees in 1964 to just over 18 million in early 2006, mainly because of the growth of the service sector and the increased employment of women.

The shift away from manufacturing employment explains in political economy terms why the modern Labour Party seems so indifferent to the plight of the industrial workers who founded it, and is more concerned with appeasing those who live off the state, as beneficiaries or employees. The facts that trade union membership is largely a public sector phenomenon, and that the unions both fund the party and sponsor Labour MPs, also explain much intrusive labour market legislation. Private sector employees tend to be well aware that such legislation threatens their employment. This contrasts with public sector employees who tend to believe that: their jobs are safe; they can go on strike with impunity (Office for National Statistics, 2006c, compares working days lost through strikes in the public and private sectors); and that increased labour costs will be met from the taxpayers' pocket.

Atkinson and all that

One last important change associated with the introduction of the ESA95 national accounting principles in 1998 is that the ESA95 accounts attempted to incorporate explicit measures of government productivity when quantifying the volume of general government current expenditure. This contrasts with the traditional pre-1998 system, which is still generally employed outside Britain, under which public sector output was measured as the price-deflated sum of its inputs, a system that rendered any meaningful calculation of factor 'productivity' in the public sector impossible. The adoption of the post-ESA95 system had no effect on the value figures for public spending but had noticeable effects on the estimates of the volume of public sector activity and the cost of providing a unit of public services. In turn, this had affected the estimate of GDP. Unfortunately, the ONS was in a position to implement this change retrospectively from only 1994 onwards, making it hard to know how comparable the published data for

Table 8 Government output per employee compared with other sectors, and comparison of government and household consumption price trends

Years	General government output per employee 1997 = 100	Annual % change	Non-oil GDP per employee 1997 = 100	Annual % change	Manufacturing output per employee 1997 = 100	Annual % change	General government consumption deflator 1997 = 100	Annual % change	Household consumption deflator 1997 = 100	Annual % change
1995	96.7	2.3	96.9	1.2	99.6	−1.0	95.1	2.2	94.7	3.3
1996	99.3	2.7	98.7	1.9	98.9	−0.8	98.2	3.3	97.6	3.1
1997	100.0	0.7	100.0	1.3	100.0	1.2	100.0	1.8	100.0	2.4
1998	100.9	0.8	102.6	2.6	100.4	0.3	102.7	2.7	102.6	2.6
1999	102.3	1.5	104.6	1.9	104.7	4.3	107.4	4.6	104.2	1.5
2000	104.0	1.6	107.2	2.5	110.2	5.3	111.7	4.0	105.6	1.3
2001	104.8	0.7	108.3	1.0	113.4	2.9	116.7	4.5	107.8	2.1
2002	106.0	1.1	110.2	1.7	116.6	2.9	123.2	5.6	109.3	1.4
2003	106.5	0.5	112.2	1.9	123.3	5.7	130.4	5.8	111.3	1.8
2004	107.3	0.8	115.2	2.6	131.9	6.9	136.2	4.4	113.0	1.5
2005	108.7	1.3	116.6	1.3	135.3	2.5	141.6	4.0	115.8	2.5

Source: ONS, 'UK Output, Income and Expenditure', first release, 25 August 2006, and ONS employment data.

before that date are with the post-1994 figures. Once the ONS had claimed that their statistics for general government current expenditure in volume terms represented a measure of government output, the next stage was for mischievous people, such as this author, to divide the output series by general government employment to see what was happening to government productivity, and to start comparing the increase in the price of providing government services with wider inflation measures.

The apparently damning results of such an exercise are presented in Table 8, which shows that the cumulative growth in government output per head since the present government took office has been only 52.5 per cent of the level in the non-oil economy as a whole (which includes the government sector) and 24.5 per cent of that achieved in manufacturing. At the same time, the cost of providing government services has risen by a cumulative 22.25 per cent more than the price of household consumption since 1997, despite the fact that the latter has been pushed up by the higher indirect taxes imposed during the early part of Labour's period in office.[1] By combining these figures, it is

---

1   It used to be believed that the cost of government services would inevitably rise relative to prices generated in the private sector, because public services are inherently less likely to benefit from technical advance than the private sector (see Baumol, 1967, for more on the 'unbalanced productivity growth' hypothesis). There was considerable justification for this view when it was first proposed. This was because the private sector was then heavily influenced by its manufacturing component – where productivity growth tends to be unusually strong – while the public sector supplied largely labour-intensive services. The reduced importance of manufacturing in countries such as the USA and Britain, and the rapid expansion of private sector services, means that it is now less easy to see any justification for an adverse relative price effect in the public sector. Statistical analyses of the relationship between the general government price deflator and other price measures, which used a time trend to pick up the relative price effect, confirmed that the rate of public sector price inflation has been above its expected rate in

possible to calculate that the same volume of government services could have been provided for some 23.75 per cent or £63.5 billion less in calendar year 2005, if public sector productivity and price discipline had matched that in the private sector. This is over and above any waste that already existed in 1997.

Newspapers started publicising such calculations and this had several consequences. Clearly the Chancellor of the Exchequer did not appreciate such comparisons between private and public sector productivity being made. The ONS then suppressed the government employment series for a couple of years, until they had time to double-check the government employment numbers. The Atkinson (2005) inquiry into the measurement of government output was set up, which kicked the government productivity issue into touch until after the May 2005 general election. A final consequence was the establishment of the UK Centre for the Measurement of Government Activity (UKCeMGA) in July 2005 as a separate directorate within the ONS.

One problem faced by Professor Atkinson was that the government's management information and control systems provided a surprisingly poor guide to its activities, presumably because civil servants are less concerned about managing their resources efficiently than private sector managers. In particular, the different ways of measuring activity showed large discrepancies, a problem already encountered with respect to employment. An early investigation into the problem of measuring government output was provided by Pritchard (2002), while the most recent figures are available in UK Centre for the Measurement of Government Activity (2005, 2006a for education and

---

recent years, even after allowing for the historic upwards drift in the public/private costs ratio.

2006b for health). All these studies revealed large discrepancies between the various attempts that have been made to measure the output of individual government 'products' such as health, education, personal social services, social security administration and fire protection services. An even more fundamental conceptual problem, however, is that it is often impossible to measure inputs and outputs properly, even in cash terms, in a highly socialised system such as health or education. One reason is that it is impossible to know the true value that consumers place on services provided free at the point of use.

Government-funded researchers are now increasingly trying to measure the output of public services using sociological techniques to measure the utility provided by them: there are parallels here with the fashionable 'economics of happiness' approach (see Box 8 in Chapter 7). The methods involved frequently seem so questionable, however, that the investigators concerned appear to be repeating the intellectual error of the Bolsheviks in 1917, and trying to reinvent the signalling properties of the price mechanism by creating a parallel bureaucratic universe, which performs the same function with massively less efficiency. It is hard to avoid the conclusion that the costs of implementing the government's Byzantine information and control systems are now far larger than the benefits they provide. The Royal Statistical Society (2003) has made a devastating critique of the way in which the government's performance indicators are compiled, and has called for a whole range of improvements, including much wider consideration of the ethics and cost efficiency of the government's obsessive-compulsive performance monitoring. Meanwhile, the task of evaluating the extent to which increased government spending has generated greater 'output' rather than being frittered away in higher costs remains an open question, given the limited quality of the available ONS data.

Annexe: Other measurement problems

The introduction of the ESA95 accounting conventions and subsequent changes not only led to noticeable differences in the way that government activity is measured, but also added tens of billions of pounds to previous official estimates of money GDP, as a result of definitional changes and developments, such as new sampling methods. The pre-1997 Conservative government's intentions with respect to the government spending and tax burdens – as set out in their last 1997 Budget, for example – are probably of interest only to antiquarians nowadays. It is still illuminating, however, to compare the spending and tax burdens for fiscal year 1997/98 – which is the last full financial year for which pre-ESA95 figures were published – as they were reported at the time and as they appear on today's definitions.

This exercise (Table 9) reveals that the reported figure for aggregate general government spending has not changed by all that much, but there have been noticeable changes to its individual components, something that strengthens the case for concentrating on wide measures of the tax and spending burdens. The main changes to the tax and spending ratios, however, have arisen from the new ways of measuring GDP, which appears to be much higher on the latest figures. The net effect of the cumulative changes to both the numerator and the denominator has been to apparently reduce the share of taxes in national output by 1.7 percentage points and the share of government spending in national output by 1.4 percentage points, compared to the

Table 9 **Comparison of pre-ESA95 definitions and most recent way of measuring general government spending in fiscal year 1997/98**

	Pre-ESA95 value (£bn)	Current value (£bn)	Difference (£bn)	Difference as a percentage of market-price GDP (current definition)
Expenditure				
General government consumption	159.2	148.8	–10.4	–1.3
Subsidies	8.2	5.4	–2.8	–0.3
Current grants to persons	101.7	105.9	4.2	0.5
Current grants abroad	5.3	0.1	–5.2	–0.7
Debt interest	28.4	29.7	1.3	0.2
Other current grants	–	13.5	13.5	1.6
General government investment	12.8	10.7	–2.1	–0.3
Stock building	0.1	0.2	0.1	0.0
Capital grants	4.3	5.4	1.1	0.1
Total general government expenditure	320.0	319.7	0.3	0.1
(Ratio of total expenditure to GDP at market prices (%))	(40.2)	(38.8)	(n/a)	(–1.4)
Receipts				
Non-oil taxes, National Insurance, etc.	293.3	289.0	–4.3	–0.5
(Ratio of non-oil taxes etc. to GDP at market prices (%))	(36.8)	(35.1)	(n/a)	(–1.7)
Rent, trading income, etc.	17.7	19.5	1.8	0.2
North Sea tax receipts	3.4	3.3	–0.1	–0.0
Taxes paid directly to EU (now excluded; see text for details)	–	5.8	5.8	0.7

Source: ONS, Financial Statistics and data bank, and author's calculations.

pre-ESA95 definitions. This illustrates the arbitrary nature of attempts to measure the burden of government and emphasises the importance of maintaining consistent definitions for purposes of international comparison and across time.

A final point before proceeding to more economic issues is that it is not only the national and government accounts which have changed dramatically in recent years. The *Budget Report*, for example, has exploded in size since 1997 – the 2006 physical Budget documentation weighed no less than 3.1 kilograms (nearly half a stone) – but has lost much of the simple factual information that characterised its predecessors, including politically sensitive figures on how the Budget tax changes affected particular income groups. Another serious loss is the once regular annual article in the ONS's *Economic Trends* showing how Britain's tax and social security burdens compare with those in other countries, which last appeared in March 1999. In addition, it is now hard to know the extent of direct EU expenditure in Britain, since this increasingly important fourth arm of government has largely gone missing from official British data sources, although quarterly figures for the taxes paid directly to the EU, such as the VAT precept, are tucked away in the ONS's *Balance of Payments*, first release (see Table H in the 30 June 2006 release; the ONS data-bank code for this item is CGDR).

3 ECONOMIC PERFORMANCE AND THE SIZE OF GOVERNMENT: EVIDENCE FROM ECONOMIC MODELS AND EMPIRICAL STUDIES

This chapter looks at the evidence on economic growth and the size of the public sector provided by macroeconomic models and other empirical studies. The underlying theoretical reasons for these results are then discussed in Chapter 4, with some additional insight into the empirical effects of public spending on growth that the theory helps to illuminate.

The government's budget constraint

Four decades ago, the author was taught the then prevalent Keynesian view that monetary policy was almost completely ineffective; the private sector of the economy was inherently unstable; the levels of public spending and taxes should be varied to offset this instability; and there was little reason to worry about the size of budget deficits – because the extra activity they generated would eventually close the initial fiscal gap. This view was tested to destruction in the early 1970s and became discredited because of the weak growth, rising unemployment, rapid inflation and massive fiscal and balance of payments deficits experienced in the mid-1970s. After this experience, economists started paying serious attention to the 'government budget constraint'. This is the fact that, under double-entry bookkeeping, public spending could only be financed through higher taxes, long-term borrowing or the potentially hyper-inflationary route of borrowing from the banking system.

The early model-based evidence

UK macroeconomic modellers burnt a lot of midnight oil over these issues following the UK economic crisis of the mid-1970s, which culminated in the December 1976 International Monetary Fund (IMF) loan. As a result, it was widely recognised, well before Mrs Thatcher became Prime Minister in May 1979, that there were a number of potential offsets to the traditional expansionary effects of budget deficits – particularly if broad money and domestic credit were being targeted as had happened under the terms of the 1969 and 1976 IMF loans – even if there was strong debate about the scale and speed of these effects.

One route through which budget deficits were found to crowd out private activity in the late 1970s was through the effects of increased bond-market funding pressure on the long-term rate of interest. This adverse effect has recently been confirmed by research from the US Federal Reserve, which estimated that a 1 percentage point rise in the projected US budget deficit to GDP ratio was associated with a 0.25 percentage point increase in the US long-term rate of interest (see Laubach, 2003; this author has found quantitatively similar effects in the British bond yield equations included in his own forecasting model). Another crowding-out effect uncovered several decades ago was the extent to which the higher inflation generated by monetised public sector deficits reduced the real values of money and other financial assets, leading to reduced consumption and investment. Once again, this is not just history, however, because some of these effects can still be found in the macroeconomic models employed by today's forecasting groups and central banks. A recent such study can be found in the technical manual describing the new Bank of England Quarterly Model (see Harrison et al., 2005: 137–9), which incorporates a distinction between the supply and the demand effects of government spending. Further examples can be found by searching other central banks' working or discussion papers, using the Bank for International Settlements (www.bis.org) as a portal. The European Central Bank (ECB), in particular, has published numerous papers, only some of which are cited here (www.ecb.int).

Warwick Macroeconomic Modelling Bureau studies

In Britain, these early results were subsequently extended by the long-running studies carried out by the Macroeconomic Modelling Bureau at the University of Warwick – which existed from 1983 to 1999. The Warwick bureau's function was to investigate the properties of the leading forecasting models of the day, including those of HM Treasury and the Bank of England, as well as those run by independent institutions such as the National Institute of Economic and Social Research (NIESR) and the London Business School (LBS). By and large, the Warwick work indicated that, after a year or so, a rise of £x in the volume of government spending produced a less than £x rise in real GDP, and in some cases was associated with an actual reduction in national output. Because government spending is a component of GDP, this implied that private sector activity was crowded out, at least on a pound-for-pound basis, in that it fell by £x or more as a result of the initial £x rise in government spending.

In addition, the Warwick studies provided useful clues as to the speed and power with which spending and taxes affect the British economy – and also to which are the most and least harmful taxes – all of which is highly relevant to the present-day discussion of these issues. The quality of the debate on the fiscal options facing Britain might be improved if the various public and independent model proprietors presently operating in the UK were to present comparable analyses using their current macroeconomic models.

Despite its age, the research carried out by the Warwick bureau also throws considerable doubt on the static calculations of the returns from raising taxes still employed by groups such as the Institute for Fiscal Studies (IFS) – for example, in their *Green Budget* reports – although this does not detract from the IFS's microeconomic research, and their website (www.ifs.org.uk) has already been recommended. To quote from page 87 of Church et al. (1993):

> In order to analyse the impact of the various fiscal policy instruments it is essential to consider both direct and indirect effects. For example, the direct effects of tax changes on government finances can be quantified through an assessment of the size of the tax base to which the tax change is to be applied, and such calculations may measure the short-run impact on government revenue quite well. However, over a period beyond the first few months following the tax change, the indirect effects through the operation of the economy as a whole come to dominate. Simulations of models of the macro-economy are the only method of quantifying the size and time profile of these indirect effects.

It is noteworthy that this refers to the conventional, largely Keynesian-inspired British models of the day, and this finding is quite independent of the Laffer-curve effects believed in by US supply-siders. The reader's attention is also drawn to the use of the word 'months' in the above quotation. One thing that has always struck the author when he has discussed these issues with politicians is the latter's absolute conviction, virtually regardless of party, that we are living in a static world in which these second-round effects never come through, despite all the evidence to the contrary. This may partly be because politicians concentrate on the short term and can easily become overwhelmed by day-to-day events. It also seems to reflect, however, a failure on the part of the economists who have studied the issue to get their knowledge across to the wider public.

Some new model simulations

The author's own macroeconomic forecasting model (see the annexe to this chapter for further description) can also be used to compare the impact of changes in taxation and government spending in both the short and the long run. Three different scenarios were run through the model in addition to the main-tenance of the status quo. First there was a 'spending shock' – a significant increase in government spending; second, a 'tax shock' – a significant increase in taxation; third, the tax and spending shocks were assumed to occur simultaneously. The scenarios are described in more detail in the annexe.

Real GDP did not vary by all that much between the different scenarios, with all the various outcomes within 0.6 percentage points of each other by 2016, although there are some notice-able differences in the first year of the simulation. The fact that boosting the volume of government expenditure by the equivalent of 1.25 per cent of real GDP only adds 0.1 per cent to national output, which is defined to include government spending, by 2016 implies that other components of GDP have been crowded out. A relatively small reduction in total GDP can mask a much larger fall in private expenditure. By 2016, each £1 billion added to the volume of government spending in the second scenario slices some £495 million off household consumption, £295 million off private investment and £255 million off net exports, for example.

Second, though inflation is widely regarded as being an essentially monetary phenomenon in the long run, this is not entirely confirmed by our simulations. The results show the level of the target Consumer Price Index (CPI) in 2016 varying by between −2.2 per cent and +3.1 per cent from the base run on the three alternative scenarios. The CPI rises by 20.25 per cent between 2005 and 2016, however, even on the base run, while the old RPIX target measure goes up by 27.25 per cent over the same period, so that these differences may not be all that large in the wider context. The short-run effects of higher indirect taxes on the CPI are powerful, but this is then partly compensated by higher interest rates.

Extra general government spending on its own is associated with slightly lower unemployment in the long run, but this is mainly because employment in the government sector is endogenous and increased public spending generates another 117,000 general government employees by 2016. Higher taxes on their own destroy jobs, and 'tax and spend' leaves the jobless total higher by 2016.

Tax receipts are also endogenous and reflect the share of the private sector – which bears the burden of taxation – in national output, in addition to the level and structure of individual tax rates. The tendency for the private sector tax base to 'slip away' when tax rates are raised means that the Public Sector Net Cash Requirement (PSNCR) initially starts as a larger share of national output in 2006/07 with higher tax rates than in the base run, but by 2016 the high-tax scenario is delivering a small PSNCR surplus, despite lower private sector expenditure and higher unemployment than in the base run. The 'pure spending' scenario raises the PSNCR/GDP ratio from 3.3 to 5.5 per cent by 2016, although 'tax and spend' reduces it to 1.9 per cent of national output.

While the long-run effects of higher taxes and public spending are already quite substantial in these simulations, it is worth noting that the increase in spending and taxation under the present Chancellor has been far larger than the small perturbations contemplated here. This could be important if the impact of tax and spending changes is non-linear as they increase in size. It is also probable that different projections for the world background would have larger effects on the UK economy than the small perturbations to the tax and spending assumptions considered in these simulations, because of the openness of the British economy. This means, in turn, that the results could well be different if a different set of projections were employed for the international economic background.

The relatively small effect of higher taxes and governmental spending on total GDP revealed by our study may also reflect weaknesses in the way that the model treats the supply side, which is difficult to model correctly, as well as the offsetting feedback through lower imports. In particular, if technical progress is embodied in capital investment, as the 'post-neo-classical endogenous growth' theories discussed in Chapter 4 suggest, then high public spending not only crowds out private investment, but also crowds out the productivity growth that is assumed to be exogenous in neo-classical theories of economic growth. This suggests that the opportunity cost of public spending may be larger when technical progress is rapid than in less dynamic eras. The conclusion is that economists still do not know enough to incorporate the effects of government spending and taxes with any precision in macroeconomic models. At this point, it is appropriate to include a quotation on the problems facing all quantitative studies in economics from Campos et al. (2005):

> Economists have long sought to develop quantitative models of economic behaviour by blending economic theory with data evidence. The task has proved an arduous one because of the nature of the economy modelled, the economic theory and the data evidence. The economy is a complicated, dynamic, non-linear, simultaneous, high-dimensional, and evolving entity; social systems alter over time; laws change; and technological innovations occur. Thus, the target is not only a moving one; it behaves in a distinctly non-stationary manner, both evolving over time and being subject to sudden and unanticipated shifts. Economic theories are highly abstract and simplified; and they also change over time with conflicting rival explanations sometimes coexisting. The data evidence is tarnished: economic magnitudes are inaccurately measured and subject to substantive revisions, and many important variables are not even observable.

These concerns apply particularly strongly to attempts to quantify the impact of government spending on economic performance, because one is trying to tease out low-frequency phenomena from poor data, which is not compiled consistently, either across time or between countries. They also explain why there is massive circumstantial evidence that pushing government spending well beyond its optimum share of GDP is damaging to economic performance, but there can never be 100 per cent proof.

Public spending and taxation: results from cross-section and panel-data studies

Model-based simulations of the effects of public spending, and how it is financed, are vitally important. This is because of the light they throw on the dynamics and detailed transmission mechanism of changes in public spending and taxation. A simplistic focus on concepts such as GDP can cause one to underestimate the damage done to the private sector in a small, open economy – such as Britain's. Model simulations tend to throw up indigestible masses of material and have been accused of confusing business cycle effects with long-term changes, although this is probably not true of contemporary macroeconomic models, which tend to have well-defined long-run properties.

The alleged weaknesses of the model-based approach mean that there is both a 'short-cut' literature, which attempts to relate economic variables directly to the tax or spending burden as measured over time in one country (see Smith, 1998, for example), as well as cross-section studies examining economic performance and public spending averaged over long periods across a number of countries. More recently, the older cross-section approach has evolved into the more sophisticated 'panel-data' methodology, which combines cross-section data for a range of countries with higher-frequency, usually annual, time-series data. The short-cut literature will not be discussed here; in part, because the simpler forms of such relationships can be considered to be no more than a 'condensed form' of the more detailed representations found in macroeconomic models.[1]

The author was responsible for one of the first crude cross-section studies three decades ago (see Smith, 1975; OECD, 1985, covers other early studies), and a number of similar investigations have been published since then, often by international bodies such as the IMF or the OECD. Unfortunately, the practical problems involved in obtaining consistent data series for a large sample of countries over a long span of years mean that fewer studies have been performed than might have been expected. These data problems also mean that the results have often proved inconclusive, and some authors have a sceptical view of the methodology concerned (see Freeman, 2001). A particularly well-known study was carried out by Professor Barro (1997), who employed a sample of roughly one hundred countries and examined the effects of a wide range of economic influences on the growth of real GDP per head. These influences included: measures of educational attainment, life expectancy, fertility rates and inflation; and more subjective indices of the extent of the rule of law, and the level of democracy; as well as the government consumption ratio. Barro's statistical findings indicated that, other things being equal, the rate of economic growth was negatively correlated with the level of output already achieved – in other words, economic maturity – and that there was a statistically significant negative effect of

---

1   Monetary economists are now using techniques such as band spectrum analysis (see Assenmacher-Wesche and Gerlach, 2006, for example). It would be interesting to apply such techniques to the relationship between public spending and national output as this may reveal that the high-frequency relationship may be positive and the, more important, low-frequency, long-run relationship negative.

government consumption on economic growth. Interestingly, the coefficient of minus 0.136 that Barro found on the government consumption ratio was close to the minus 0.133 that the author had discovered more than two decades earlier, suggesting that the effect may be stable.

Some critics have suggested that there may have been statistical problems (to do with simultaneity) in some of the earlier cross-section studies, which could have biased the estimated effects of government spending on growth, although this probably does not apply to the techniques employed by Professor Barro. More recent research, however, suggests that the bias has been towards under- rather than over-representation. For example, the OECD (2003) reported the results of a 'panel-data' study using data for 21 developed countries over the years 1971–98. This came up with an almost identical negative coefficient of 0.15, when the effect of the government spending ratio on economic growth was considered in isolation. The OECD found, however, that public spending had a coefficient of +0.19 – which seems on the low side given that government spending is included in GDP – but taxes had a negative coefficient of 0.44, when spending and taxes were included separately. This implies that tax-financed expenditures have an overall negative impact on growth of 0.25 percentage points or 1.75 times the negative spending coefficient estimated by Barro.

To be on the safe side, Table 10 applies Barro's lower estimate of a 0.136 negative impact of the government consumption/GDP ratio to the figures in Table 1, using the change in the public spending ratio between 1960 and 2005 to generate the estimated impact on economic growth. This illustrative calculation provides some feel for the order of magnitude of the effects involved, but

Table 10 **Estimated effects on economic growth of increase in public spending since 1960**

	Change in public spending burden 1960–2005 (%)	Estimated impact on annual economic growth (%)	How much higher output would have been in 2005 with 1960 spending levels (%)
Australia	13.2	−1.8	123
Austria	0.9	−0.1	5
Belgium	21.2	−3.0	278
Canada	8.1	−1.1	64
France	19.8	−2.8	246
Germany	15.0	−2.1	155
Ireland	6.1	−0.9	50
Italy	18.1	−2.5	204
Japan	19.4	−2.7	232
Netherlands	15.6	−2.2	166
New Zealand	−1.3	+0.2	−9
Norway	17.1	−2.4	191
Spain	19.2	−2.7	232
Sweden	23.4	−3.3	331
Switzerland	23.2	−3.2	313
United Kingdom	10.4	−1.5	95
United States	5.3	−0.7	37
Unweighted average	13.8	−1.9	160

Source: Author's calculations, OECD and IMF, as quoted in note to Table 1.*
* The change in the public spending burden has been 'break-corrected' to allow for discrepancies in overlap years. The figures should, however, be regarded as highly approximate only. A particular concern is that the figures for 1960 and 2005 may have been distorted by business cycle effects, and it would have been better to do the calculation with five- or ten-year averaged data if such had been available.

should be regarded as no more than a rough approximation. One reason is that Professor Barro's definition of the government sector may differ from that in Table 1, although the use of the change in the spending ratio, rather than its level, should reduce this problem if the items excluded by Barro are a broadly constant share of GDP. Another problem is that the adverse effects of a rising government spending burden are almost certainly non-linear, and grow more than proportionately beyond a certain point. It is also conceivable that the adverse effects of economic maturity would have offset the growth-enhancing effects of a smaller public sector if countries had become richer faster, although this depends on the theoretical model employed, an issue that is returned to later. The figures in Table 10 are therefore no more than rough-and-ready estimates. The very large effects shown in the final column are, however, probably more plausible than they might appear at first sight because they reflect a combination of the big increases in the size of the typical public sector over the past 45 years and the power of compound interest over such a long period: that is because government expenditure affects *growth* and loss of growth compounds each year. The estimates are also consistent with the crowding out long observed in conventional macroeconomic forecasting models, despite the fact that Barro concentrated on the long-term supply-side influences on growth whereas the older macroeconomic models tended to emphasise shorter-term demand-side and business-cycle effects.

Annexe: The author's macroeconomic model

This annexe describes the author's econometric forecasting model 'WINMOD', which has been in continuous existence since 1984. The model contains 133 quarterly economic variables, of which 71 are predicted using econometric relationships (a model printout PowerPoint presentation and a technical manual are available from www.xxxbeaconxxx@btinternet.com). In carrying out the simulations, it was assumed that the world background, which is also endogenous, remained the same. WINMOD is near to being what engineers would call a 'closed system', and the sterling index, short- and long-term interest rates, narrow and broad money, the price of government expenditure, welfare benefits and government debt interest are all endogenous within its predictive framework. The feedbacks from these variables into the rest of the model explain some of the results. For example, increased budget deficits in the first year lead to higher debt servicing costs and increased deficits in future years.

Each of the model simulations discussed above required only a matter of seconds to perform. The 'base run' replicates the forecasts contained in Williams de Broë's May 2006 *Quarterly Interest Rate Outlook* report, which was published on 12 May 2006. The forecasts in that document should not be taken literally as a guide to the future outlook, one reason being that the UK national accounts were rebased on 30 June 2006, so that the model will have been entirely rebuilt and the base-run forecasts will be obsolete by the time that this is read. This does not matter for the purpose at hand, however, which is to illustrate the marginal differences to a central forecast that occur when tax and government spending assumptions are being tweaked, and to bring out the complexity of some of the results once allowance is made for the dynamic feedbacks involved.

One way of regarding this analysis is as being what 'Cliometricians' would call a 'counter-factual' designed to see what would have happened if Gordon Brown had adopted different policies in his March 2006 Budget. The 'spending shock' scenarios assume that the volume of general government current expenditure was increased by 5 per cent in 2006 Q2 and remained persistently 5 per cent above the path assumed in the 'base run'. Such step changes are not realistic but are used in model simulations because it is easier to analyse the results. The assumed jump in general government spending was equivalent to adding nearly £12.25 billion to the volume of government spending in 2006/07, measured in 2002 prices, and £14.25 billion in cash terms. In fiscal year 2005/06, general government current expenditure represented only 53 per cent of total government spending – which also includes investment, transfers and debt interest, among other items – and 24.8 per cent of the basic-price measure of real GDP. This means that the spending shock involved represents 1.2 per cent of total GDP.

The 'tax shock' scenarios examine what happens if all the various tax rates incorporated in the model – VAT, income tax, corporation tax, employees' and employers' National Insurance contributions and the average percentage rates of specific duty and other current taxes – had been raised by 1p in the pound from 2006 Q2 onwards, compared with their levels in the base run. This assumption adds 6.1 per cent to the weighted average tax rate in 2006/07, and on a purely static calculation might be expected to add some £28.75 billion in cash terms to tax receipts in 2006/07, which is twice the size of the *ex ante* expenditure shock. The second-round effects come to dominate so rapidly, however, that cash receipts are no higher in 2006/07 than in the base run, and the rise in the ratio of taxes to GDP is entirely the result of lower nominal GDP. Clearly, the effects of different taxes are not identical and a 1p across-the-board hike was primarily chosen for reasons of presentational simplicity. There is no limit to the number of scenarios that could be generated using slightly different assumptions.

The final 'tax and spending' shock combined the assumption of a 5 per cent hike in the volume of general government expenditure with the 1p tax increase scenario. In other words, it represented both 'tax and spend', rather than each considered separately.

4 ECONOMIC PERFORMANCE AND THE SIZE OF GOVERNMENT: ECONOMIC THEORY

Here we look at the contribution of economic theory to our understanding of the impact of tax and spend policies on economic growth. There will be some further discussion of empirical evidence in the context of the application of empirical studies to the testing of the theories.

The Ricardian Equivalence Theorem

One result of the model-based research described in the previous chapter is that it was recognised some three decades ago that the stimulatory Keynesian effects of budget deficits could be offset by their crowding-out effects on private investment, household consumption and net exports, although there was, of course, much debate about the precise speeds, magnitudes and transmission mechanisms involved. In this context, it is interesting that the present Chancellor, Gordon Brown, has never tried to justify budget deficits using Keynesian arguments.

The rational expectations revolution of the 1970s led to a still stronger rejection of the view that budget deficits stimulated the economy. One turning point here was the publication of Barro's article on the Ricardian Equivalence Theorem in 1974, although it took some time before the importance of this article was recognised in the UK policy debate. Barro argued that

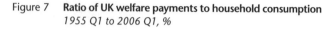

Figure 7   **Ratio of UK welfare payments to household consumption**
1955 Q1 to 2006 Q1, %

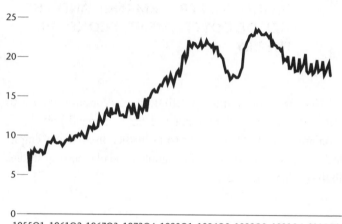

Note: The chart follows the official ONS definition of tax credits, whereby a significant part is treated as a negative tax, not a benefit.

rational individuals would anticipate the future increase in taxes required to finance budget deficits, would realise that they were worse off as a result, and hence would cut back their consumption immediately.

The Ricardian equivalence approach remains controversial for various reasons. For example, government spending on welfare benefits gives money to a sector of the population who tend to consume their entire income (Figure 7), while taxes tend to fall on people with more disposable income and a greater scope for discretionary switches between spending and saving. This suggests that Ricardian equivalence may apply only to the non-welfare-financed element of consumption, and not to consumption as a whole.

Despite these reservations, there is now considerable evidence from international studies, such as OECD (2003), that a high proportion of any increase in public borrowing is indeed neutralised by an offsetting shift in private sector savings. This evidence applies even if one might be agnostic as to whether this reflects, first, a rational expectations phenomenon on Barro lines or, alternatively, the upward pressure on long-term interest rates caused by official debt sales (Smith, 2006). Whatever the precise mechanism involved, an important implication of the empirical finding that private savings change to offset any stimulatory impact of budget deficits is that there exists a destabilising negative feedback between the budget deficit and private sector activity and the tax base. This feedback means that low household savings, buoyant consumption and strong tax receipts are likely to be observed when there are government surpluses, and that the converse applies if the public finances are being managed imprudently, or people come to believe that they are likely to be managed imprudently because of political developments. The possibility that these feedbacks can induce either a vicious or a virtuous circle, depending on whether the fiscal deficit is growing or being cut, may explain some of the findings of the fiscal-stabilisation literature, discussed later in this chapter. It ought to be a serious policy concern in Britain, given the deterioration in the government's financial position in recent years, the recent slowdown in household consumption and the associated tendency for tax revenues to undershoot official forecasts.

The damage caused by taxes
Taxes destroy property rights

It is now appropriate to concentrate a little more on to the subject of taxation, bearing in mind, as always, that increased public spending inevitably implies some combination of higher taxes, increased long-term borrowing or inflationary finance. It is also worth noting that the impact of taxes operates in several different ways.

The first such way is that all taxes expropriate the fruits of capital, labour or enterprise, and transfer real resources from the people who created the wealth to those who did not. This 'plunder' (*spoliation* in the original French), to use Bastiat's terminology, represents a fundamental injustice, which turns all taxpayers into quasi-slaves who work without reward for many days of the year, and explains why a moral state should feel inhibited in the degree to which it levies taxation, particularly if the tax structure is not designed to minimise the costs of compliance and may be arbitrary in its imposition.

To an economist, however, one striking aspect of all taxes, and also much government regulation, is that they destroy individuals' property rights. In particular, taxes and inappropriate regulation expropriate either people's capital or the return on their capital, including the human capital built up by education, training and a willingness to accept the social discipline of the workplace. Arguably this represents a form of legally enforced extortion, which is why moral governments should always feel inhibited about the imposts that they impose on their citizens. Moreover, it is widely accepted in economic history and development economics that capital formation of any kind will not be undertaken if there is a risk of arbitrary expropriation, perhaps as the result of tyranny, a collapse of law and order, or the chaos of war. A stable, but high, tax and regulatory structure will have serious economic costs, although a largely free-market economy will adjust to minimise the damage, just as it adjusts to high energy costs, for example. A constantly changing and capriciously unpredictable tax and regulatory regime recreates, however, in a bloodless way, the breakdown of fundamental property rights that is normally found in periods of civil commotion, war or primitive barbarism. Unfortunately, this adverse uncertainty effect has become increasingly important in Britain since 1997 because the tax system has become more complex and unstable, and subject to retrospective legislation.

Adverse microeconomic effects of higher taxes

Taxes have important implications for the efficient functioning of the economy at the microeconomic level of individual producers and consumers. One set of costs is the compliance costs involved in having to fill in tax forms and meet the regulations concerned. This has two elements: one is the unpaid time devoted to these activities (this loss of valuable time is ignored in the national accounts); the other is the cost of employing accountants and tax advisers, which is treated as adding to GDP![1] The other set of hidden costs arises because taxes drive a wedge between the price signals perceived by consumers and those received by producers, and give rise to substantial dead-weight losses of real economic welfare (see Figure 8 below). Thus, as Lightfoot (2005)

---

1   The American Enterprise Institute website, www.aei.org, contains a number of useful papers on compliance costs, and the institute recently held a conference on the subject. There seems to be rather less British material.

Figure 8   **Deadweight loss from higher taxes**

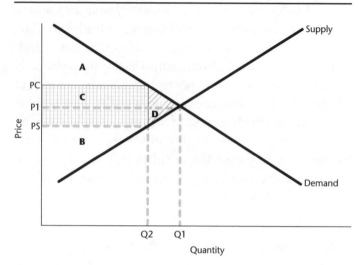

Figure 8 illustrates what happens when a flat-rate consumption tax is imposed on a product. Supply falls from Q1 to Q2, the price to the consumer rises from P1 to PC, and the price received by the producer falls from P1 to PS. The revenue received by the government corresponds to the area C on the diagram. Both the consumer surplus A and the producer surplus B are smaller than before. The area D represents the dead-weight cost of taxation, and represents the utility that has simply disappeared as a result of the tax being imposed.

has pointed out, the US Congressional Budget Office (CBO) has reported that the 'typical estimates of the economic cost of a dollar of tax revenue range from 20 cents to 60 cents over and above the revenue raised', proportions that would indicate dead-weight losses of £90 billion to £270 billion in fiscal 2005/06 if applied to UK non-oil tax receipts, or 8.5 to 25.5 per cent of factor cost GDP.

Because of the dead-weight costs of taxation (which, in theory, grow with the square of the marginal tax rate) most economists

Table 11 **Taxes as a percentage of gross income for non-retired households by quintile groups,* 2004/05**

	Quintile groups of non-retired households					All non-retired households
	Bottom	2nd	3rd	4th	Top	
Percentages						
Direct taxes						
Income tax[†]	4.3	8.9	11.8	14.3	19.0	14.3
Employees' NIC	2.9	4.8	5.7	6.2	4.8	5.1
Council tax and NI rates[‡]	3.7	3.2	2.8	2.3	1.6	2.3
All direct taxes	10.9	16.9	20.2	22.8	25.3	21.7
All indirect taxes	26.3	19.4	16.7	14.0	10.2	14.5
All taxes	37.3	36.3	36.9	36.7	35.5	36.3

* Households are ranked by equivalised disposable income.

† After deducting tax credits and tax relief at source on life assurance premiums.

‡ After deducting discounts, council tax benefit and rates rebates.

have always argued that flat-rate proportional taxes are the least damaging, because they are the least distortionary at the margin, where all economic decisions are made. It is also striking how close the UK tax system is to being flat or even mildly regressive (see Table 11) once indirect taxes are allowed for as well as direct ones, although the official calculations reproduced in this table exclude employers' National Insurance contributions, which are arguably just another tax on labour income and affect different groups to varying degrees (the source for these figures is Jones, 2006). A flat tax that involves a high marginal rate still distorts economic incentives and creates dead-weight losses, however, and a progressive system with sufficiently low marginal rates may be preferable to a flat tax with a high marginal rate, although this almost certainly requires a lower spending burden in the first place.

It is argued in Chapter 8 that a flat tax which does not allow for any deductions or a tax-free threshold may be desirable from a political-economy perspective, because it reinforces the link between taxation and representation that is a necessary condition for a properly functioning democracy. Eliminating thresholds also has the practical benefits, however, that it makes the tax cheap to administer and easy to comply with. The disincentive effects created by a flat tax without thresholds are not altered by inflation, and are less exacerbated by the regional differences in living costs discussed in Chapter 5, for example. In many taxation systems, changes in nominal earnings (but not real earnings) move some individuals into higher tax brackets when their real income has not changed, a phenomenon known as 'bracket creep'. With a flat tax, there are no 'brackets' to creep into when nominal wages change with inflation, and individuals pay a higher real tax bill if and only if their real wage increases. The British situation is different because income tax thresholds are generally raised in line with inflation each year and it is real fiscal drag associated with higher real earnings pushing an ever-growing share of the workforce into the top 40 per cent marginal rate of income tax which contributes to the buoyancy of the revenue. The disincentive effects of this development are considered later.

The current vogue for flat-rate income taxes seems to represent a rediscovery of ideas that arguably go back to Victorian economists such as Alfred Marshall, and his successors such as Ramsey (1927), a clear account of whose ideas can be found in Minford (2006). This does not detract, however, from the apparent success of the flat-rate systems that have been implemented in many former communist countries in central and eastern Europe. An excellent and thorough review of the issues concerned can be found in Heath (2006a), which probably represents the best account of flat-rate taxation available on either side of the Atlantic. Unfortunately, the Keynesian revolution of the 1930s meant that the earlier concern over the adverse microeconomic effects of taxes became distinctly unfashionable for several decades, which is why the flat-tax movement appears so innovative today. The first serious attack on the post-Keynesian conventional wisdom – that the level and structure of taxes did not matter for output and employment – was launched in the 1970s by US supply-siders such as Art Laffer and the late Bob Bartley in the *Wall Street Journal* (see Roberts, 1989). The commentators concerned applied a standard neo-classical microeconomic analysis to the specific problems of analysing the effects of the tax burden on economic decisions. The Taxpayers' Alliance has mounted many of the most important papers on supply-side economics on its website (www. taxpayersalliance.com; click on 'Issues'), providing an invaluable source for people interested in these matters.

Supply-side economics

The main practical implication of the revival and extension of traditional neo-classical concerns by US supply-siders are as follows:

- There are good theoretical reasons – over and above the macroeconomic model-based evidence – for believing that the effects of taxes are larger and more rapid than the conventional wisdom suggests, particularly if people anticipate the effect of pre-announced, or cynically anticipated, tax changes in a manner consistent with rational expectations.

- Once it is accepted that higher taxes can reduce aggregate supply as well as total demand, many of the traditional ideas for controlling the economy lose their power or otherwise become invalid. The extent to which this is true depends on the relative size and speed of the supply and demand effects, and is ultimately an empirical question.
- In particular, tax-financed public spending is not neutral in its effects on output and prices, as the traditional demand-based approach assumes, because of the adverse effects on aggregate supply from the reduced incentives to work, invest and take risks.
- The spatial consequences of a high tax burden imply that the supply of tradable goods will move from high-tax to low-tax economies over time, a process known as 'hollowing out' in Germany. This should be a major concern in Britain now that this country's tax burden is rising compared with that in other industrial countries (see Figure 9), let alone when compared with such emergent economic superpowers as China.
- The possibility that total supply may be at least as flexible as effective demand means that supply-side economists should have strong reservations about the fashionable 'output gap' approach to forecasting inflation. This has serious implications for the Conventional Theoretical Macroeconomic Model, which appears to underlie the approach to forecasting inflation employed by many of the world's leading central banks (see Smith, 2006).
- The supply-side approach has close affinities with the real business cycle (RBC) literature, which examines the effect of technology 'shocks' such as the invention of the Internet on the supply of national output (see *Oxford Review of Economic Policy*,

1997, for more on the RBC approach). The mathematical models developed by the RBC school can readily cope with the effects of a tax hike, if this is treated as the equivalent of an adverse technology shock (MacGrattan, 1994).

- The supply-siders have also claimed that low-tax economies tend to have higher real exchange rates than high-tax ones, because the former represent a more desirable home for human and financial capital. This may explain why the US dollar has frequently proved to be far stronger against currencies such as the euro than many pundits expected.
- The supply-side approach also implies that a high tax burden compared with one's trading partners will lower the employment rate for any given level of national output, but that this effect will be disproportionately powerful in the internationally trading sectors of the economy, such as manufacturing. This is why the private sectors of high-tax economies tend to be relatively short on steelworkers and relatively long on aromatherapists, for example, provided that the level of unemployment benefits is sufficiently meagre to allow the labour market to clear (otherwise there is likely to be a high level of unemployment, although this may be disguised by burgeoning public sector payrolls). Given that recorded productivity growth tends to be faster in manufacturing than elsewhere (see Table 8), this switch of labour resources away from industry into public and private services could help explain why open economies with large public sectors seem to grow relatively slowly, although this may also be because the official statisticians find it easier to measure the output of 'widgets' than of social services, for example.

Figure 9   **Difference between smoothed UK and OECD tax burdens**
1964 Q1 to 2006 Q1, %

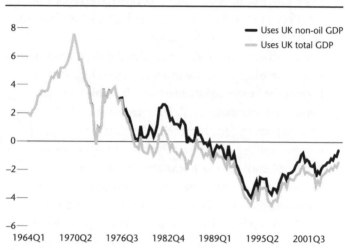

Note: GDP concept employed is market-price measure. UK tax burden is centred four-quarter average of non-oil and EU taxes, OECD is interpolated annual data. OECD figure also includes current non-tax receipts, which amount to some 2–2.5 per cent of GDP in the UK. This means that the absolute difference may overstate the UK advantage by a roughly similar amount.

Competing theories of economic growth

It should be apparent by now that there is a serious disjuncture between what economists have learnt about the consequences of tax-and-spend policies and the terms of the current British political debate. It remains possible, however, that the adverse effects of excessive public spending have been underestimated because so many researchers have employed a 'neo-classical' model of economic growth rather than the competing 'post-neo-classical endogenous growth' approach. The two theories differ because it is assumed that technical progress proceeds at a steady rate over time – like manna from heaven – in the neo-classical approach, while the endogenous growth school believes that technical innovation has to be embodied in new capital equipment.

The two approaches, in turn, lead to different hypotheses about the effects of non-productive government spending on economic growth. In particular, neo-classical theory implies that, while the level of national output would be adversely affected by excessive government spending, future growth would not be affected once the government spending burden had stabilised at a particular ratio, regardless of how high that ratio was. This is something that neo-classicists have used to explain Sweden's relatively satisfactory performance by Continental standards, for example.[2] In contrast, endogenous growth theory implies that a permanently faster increase in real GDP would result from a reduction in the tax and spending ratios, because of the extent to which technical progress was embodied in new private sector capital formation, which had previously been crowded out by a large government sector. One thing both schools agree on is that, empirically, there is a near one-to-one negative relationship between the share of government spending in GDP and the share of private sector capital formation, so that the debate is predominantly over the consequences of this phenomenon.

A clear account of the different approaches can be found in Alfonso et al. (2005), who also summarise the results of a number of previous empirical studies on the effect of government spending and taxes on economic performance, but do not present estimates of their own – while Snowden's interview with Barro's erstwhile co-author Xavier Sala-i-Martin summarises the current state

---

[2]   Although the fact that Sweden has also sharply reduced its spending and tax burdens may be a better explanation, as was argued in the first chapter.

of play in growth theory (Snowden, 2006). Minford and Wang (2006) also set out the existing research on the effects of taxes on growth and make the following distinction between 'activist' and 'incentivist' views of the growth process, before presenting empirical results that favour the incentivist approach:

> In the activist case, growth is caused by public spending on desirable elements, with no effects from taxation. Public spending on these variables being a choice arising from the political process, we can regard it as exogenous. There may be feedback from the economy's behaviour onto these variables but it is uncertain in direction and takes a long time.

In the incentivist view, growth is caused by incentives and thus by taxation. The level of public spending on desirable elements is now irrelevant. The level of taxation is determined by public choices and is now exogenous for the same reasons as above. Taxation is usually a side-effect of choices to spend public money on publicly chosen objectives, it is no less the result of policy choice. (ibid.: 2)

An important, but rather older, paper dealing with the effects of taxes on economic growth was produced by Becsi (1996), who applied an endogenous growth model to explain why the growth performance of individual US states differed so much over the period 1961–92. The USA provides an ideal test bed for such panel-data studies because of the large number of states; their high degree of fiscal autonomy (see Laubach, 2005, for a fuller account of the US system); the fact that they are in a currency union; and the good quality of the US statistics. Becsi found that it was possible to explain more than 60 per cent of the growth differences between the 50 US states used in his study in terms of three variables:

- Relative income at the start, which allowed for the tendency of poorer states to catch up, as neo-classical theory suggests should happen.
- The relative tax burden in each state.
- A measure of the regressivity of the tax system, on the basis that more progressive tax systems tended to be more distortionary at the margin.

Becsi's statistical analysis confirmed the endogenous growth theory's claim that a high and progressive state tax burden had permanent adverse effects on the growth rate, as well as on the level of a state's output. Becsi also discovered that these effects appeared to be stronger in the second half of the data period, which is what one might expect as a result of improving mobility and communications. Although as a US author writing in the mid-1990s Becsi naturally did not consider the issue, his research also implies that the adverse effects of a high national tax burden might be exacerbated in Europe by European Monetary Union (EMU). This is because EMU made tax costs transparent across the Eurozone and, together with the new competition from the East, this helps explain the current French paranoia about 'social dumping'.

The importance of this issue meant that an attempt to distinguish between the neo-classical and endogenous growth schools in the context of the effect of government spending on growth was performed by the European Central Bank (ECB) economists De Avila and Strauch in 2003. The ECB authors attempted to take advantage of the different time-series implications of the neo-classical and endogenous growth approaches, and used an extensive panel of European national data from 1960 to 2001.

Unfortunately, their empirical results were not conclusive, although they did find that government spending crowded out activity over the business cycle, and capital formation in the long run. Their inconclusive results almost certainly reflect the difficulty of measuring the concepts involved in practice, given the complexity of tax systems and the limitations of the official statistics.

The fact, however, that it remains unclear from the empirical research whether the adverse effect of non-productive government spending is, first, mainly on the level of activity or, alternatively, whether excessive public spending leads to permanently lower growth poses problems for anyone attempting to undertake a cost–benefit analysis of the effects of today's 'big governments'. This is because the discounted net present value of the damage done will tend to be larger in the latter case. On balance, it seems as if the tide of opinion is now starting to flow increasingly towards the post-neo-classical endogenous growth approach and towards the view that excessive public spending and taxation can have adverse consequences not just for the level of activity but for growth. This is important. It means that a given increase in the public sector will lead not just to a decrease in national income but to further decreases in each successive year (see Figure 10).

Table 10 in Chapter 3 not only suggests that the effects of the increased public spending experienced in most countries since the early 1960s have been immense in terms of the output forgone, but also goes some way towards explaining why the former *Wirtschaftswunder* economies of Japan, France, Spain, Italy and Germany have slowed down so abruptly since the 1960s, and also why the relative – but not the absolute – growth performances of the mature British and American economies have improved.

Figure 10 **Effects of tax-financed public spending on economic growth**

Effects in neo-classical model

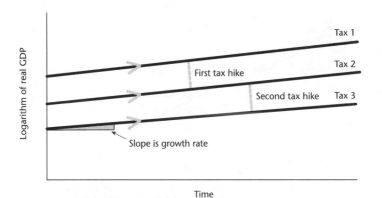

Effects in post-neo-classical endogenous growth model

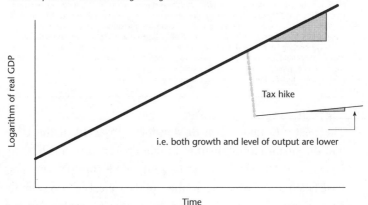

Because high levels of government spending strongly crowd out private capital formation – a result that is found repeatedly in cross-section and panel-data studies – its adverse effects on growth are noticeably stronger in endogenous growth models than they are in neo-classical ones (compare Figures 10A and 10B).

Figure 11 **Ratio of UK real GDP to OECD real GDP and fitted trends**
1960 Q1 to 2006 Q1, %

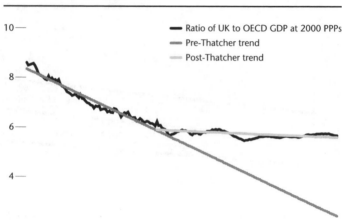

Note: The chart shows the ratio of UK real GDP at market prices to its OECD counterpart, using data back to 1960 Q1. The figures have been expressed so that the vertical axis shows the share of OECD GDP accounted for by the UK measured at 2000 purchasing power parities. This share was 5.7 per cent in 2005, for example. The level of UK real GDP in 2006 Q1 was 135 per cent up on the pre-Thatcher trend, and a trivial and statistically insignificant 1.3 per cent up on the Thatcher one. The improvement in Britain's relative performance largely reflects the slowdown in our OECD partners, and the figures should be regarded as illustrative, rather than precise. The chart does, however, provide some 'feel' for the potentially large size of the effects involved.

The relatively minor growth slowdown observed in the USA and the small improvement in Britain appear to be a tribute to Reagan and Thatcher (see Crafts, 2001, and Figure 11), who may have failed to roll back the frontiers of the state, but also seem to have prevented, for a while, the further sharp rise that has done so much damage to some other countries.

This can be seen from Table 12, which somewhat crudely compares the growth numbers in the author's 1975 article with

Table 12 **The OECD growth slowdown and the estimated effects of growth in public spending since 1960**

	Annual growth in real GDP 1961–72 (%)	Annual growth in real GDP 1995–2005 (%)	Growth deceleration (–) between the two periods	Forecast growth slowdown from Table 7	Annual growth in real GDP 2001–05 (%)
Australia	5.4	3.6	–1.8	–1.8	3.1
Austria	5.0	2.1	–2.9	–0.1	1.3
Belgium	4.8	2.1	–2.7	–3.0	1.5
Canada	5.5	3.3	–2.2	–1.1	2.6
France	5.8	2.1	–3.7	–2.8	1.6
Germany	4.5	1.3	–3.2	–2.1	0.7
Ireland	4.0	7.6	3.6	–0.9	5.3
Italy	4.8	1.4	–3.4	–2.5	0.7
Japan	10.1	1.3	–8.8	–2.7	1.3
Netherlands	5.6	2.2	–3.4	–2.2	0.8
Spain	6.9	3.2	–3.7	–2.7	3.1
Sweden	3.7	2.8	–0.9	–3.3	2.1
Switzerland	4.1	1.3	–2.8	–3.2	0.9
United Kingdom	2.9	2.8	–0.1	–1.5	2.3
United States	4.4	3.3	–1.1	–0.7	2.6
Unweighted average	5.2	2.7	–2.5	–2.0	1.9

Sources: Smith (1975) and OECD, *Economic Outlook*, June 2005, Annexe Table 1, and author's calculations.

the averages for the last decade, and also the extent to which the difference between the two is associated with the estimated effects of higher public spending. Clearly, many factors determine long-run growth rates, other than the government spending ratio, including: demographics, the extent of regulation, and institutional changes, such as trade rules. There does appear, however, to be some correspondence between the growth decelerations in the countries considered and the increased size of the state, and it is possible that these are somewhat larger than Barro's coefficient (see Chapter 3) would suggest (a coefficient of 0.2 would appear to fit the data better, while the highest coefficient that appears in the published research, to the author's knowledge, is 0.4). The final column of Table 12 shows the average growth rate over the past five years. A comparison of this column with the 1995–2005 averages shows disturbing signs of a further slowdown in every country shown, apart from Japan, which was unchanged at a mere 1.3 per cent. This deceleration might be a business cycle phenomenon, even if the traditional four- or five-year business cycle should have cancelled out over the period considered here. It is also conceivable that slow growth reflects the disruptive effects of increased geopolitical uncertainty in recent years. If this is not the case, many European economies have major problems on their hands because they appear to have largely gone *ex growth*. There is room for concern as to whether social cohesion can be maintained in such societies.

Meanwhile, Table 13, which corresponds to Table 2.8 in OECD (2003) cited earlier but deals with the level of, rather than the rate of growth in, real GDP per capita, helps explain why current high tax-and-spend policies have not done more noticeable damage to Britain's growth rate until now. In particular, it looks as if the once-and-for-all gains from the move towards the lower and more stable inflation that resulted from the granting of operational independence to the Bank of England have offset the adverse consequences of a rising UK tax burden so far. The MPC has done such a good job since May 1997, however, that these one-off gains from taming inflation have probably now been exhausted. This means that any adverse supply-side consequences of the British government's big spending policies are likely to come through unabated from now on, even if they have not done so previously. It seems appropriate to conclude this section with a direct quote

Table 13 **Estimated impact of changes in institutional or policy factors on GDP per capita***

Variable	Impact on output per working-age person (%)[†]		
	Effect via economic efficiency	Effect via investment	Overall effect
Inflation rate (fall of 1%)		0.4 to 0.5	0.4 to 0.5
Variability of inflation (1% fall in Standard Deviation of Inflation)	2.0		2.0
Tax burden[‡] (increase of 1%)	–0.3	–0.3 to –0.4	–0.6 to –0.7
Business research & development intensity[‡] (increase of 0.1%)	1.2		1.2
Trade exposure[‡] (increase of 10%)	4.0		4.0

Source: OECD (2003), Table 2.8, p. 88.

* The values reported in this table are the estimated long-run effects on output per working-age person of a given policy change. The range reported reflects the values obtained in different specifications of the growth equation.

† The direct effect refers to the impact on output per capita over and above any potential influence on the accumulation of physical capital. The indirect effect refers to the combined impact of the variable on the investment rate and, by that channel, on output per capita.

‡ Percentage of GDP.

from OECD (2003: 17) summarising its research into the effects of the government sector on economic growth:

> There is some support to the notion that the overall size of governments in the economy may reach levels that impair growth. Although expenditure on health, education and research clearly sustains living standards in the long

run, and transfers help to meet social goals, all have to be financed and high levels of taxation, as well as high government deficits, crowd out resources that could be used to raise growth potential. For a given level of taxation moreover, higher direct as opposed to indirect taxes further weaken growth potential. On the expenditure side, transfers, as opposed to government consumption and – even more so – investment, could lead to lower output per capita.

The fiscal stabilisation literature

The evidence so far suggests that there is a disjuncture between, first, the information that economists have gleaned from model simulations and panel-data studies about the adverse effects of excessive public spending and, second, the political debate in many EU countries, in which the participants treat government expenditure as a painlessly financed free good. A comparison of the first and last columns of Table 10 in Chapter 3, which shows a near-halving of the unweighted average annual growth rate from 5.2 per cent between 1961 and 1972 to 2.7 per cent between 1995 and 2005, also suggests that these are not small issues, since the difference accumulates to 82.5 per cent of real national output over a 25-year generation. At some stage, there is likely to be a serious crisis precipitated by high public spending and low growth. The issue that will then have to be faced in many European nations, including Britain, is whether their deteriorating public finances can be turned around without an emergency public spending freeze or real reductions (as distinct from the phoney cuts in notional future spending plans that politicians and bureaucrats prefer). The risk associated with politicians trying to tax their way out of structural budget deficits is that it is easy to overshoot the point where the effect of higher taxes becomes perverse, and higher taxes induce a private sector supply withdrawal and an implosion of the tax base. This is quite possibly what happened in Japan in the 1990s and early 2000s. Meanwhile, there is the conundrum of whether politicians who have denied that they intend to raise taxes before an election but have done so by stealth afterwards have a democratic mandate for their policies.

The widespread international concern about the sustainability of 'big government' policies, especially on the scale being practised in Europe, means that there is a growing literature that analyses the factors that determine the success of official attempts to stabilise the public finances. A good introduction to the political economy and other issues involved can be found in Snowden (2004). In the fiscal stabilisation literature two types of fiscal adjustment package are usually identified. 'Type 1' fiscal adjustments implement government expenditure cuts and reductions in transfer payments and public sector wages and employment, while 'Type 2' adjustments depend mainly on tax increases and cuts in public investment. Independent international bodies, such as the IMF, which frequently have to bail out errant governments, all seem to agree that only Type 1 adjustments achieve a lasting improvement in the budget deficit. In addition, Type 1 retrenchments seem to expand national output and boost competitiveness. Type 2 adjustments appear, however, to have backfired in nearly every country that has tried them, leading to a worse budget deficit and reduced economic activity. Support for these statements is provided by the research of Giudice et al. (2003), and the numerous other studies cited therein, which provides a wide-ranging empirical analysis based on the experience of many European economies since the

1970s (Briotti, 2005, provides another recent survey of the fiscal consolidation literature). Against this background, it is striking that the only form of fiscal adjustment usually on offer, even from so-called 'conservative' politicians, is of the perversely damaging Type 2 variety. This seems to be an example of a situation in which the political realities lead to an outcome that is perverse when viewed from the perspectives of economic rationallity and the welfare of society as a whole, even if this should not surprise those who understand public choice theory (Tullock et al., 2000).

A good example of recent ECB research into the practicability of cutting government spending can be found in papers by Schuknecht and Tanzi (2005a, 2005b) and more recently by Hauptmeier et al. (2006), which examined the experience of 22 industrialised countries over the past two decades. Their research demonstrated that, contrary to common belief, several previously high-spending countries were able to reduce the ratio of government spending to GDP by remarkable amounts, with six countries managing cutbacks of over 10 percentage points, and another four by between 5 and 10 percentage points. Furthermore, these ambitious reformers do not seem to have suffered from these large reductions, either in a macroeconomic sense or in terms of reduced social welfare. On the contrary, ambitious expenditure reforms appeared to coincide with improvements in fiscal, economic, human development and institutional indicators, even if it takes time for these benefits to accrue. In addition, the unfavourable effects of enhanced fiscal parsimony on income distribution appear to be small, and are mitigated in absolute terms by faster economic growth. Such research suggests that 'big government' policies are not only perverse from an economic standpoint but are also keeping the people that they are ostensibly intended to help poorer than they need be. Governments should not simply try to bolster the income of poor people in the current period but should instead attempt to maximise the net present value of their entire lifetime real income streams. This can be done by policies that promote less government spending and thus higher growth.[3]

Good, and bad, buys in taxation

All taxes destroy individual property rights and discourage effort, risk-taking and investment in physical, financial and human capital. There appear to be significant differences, however, between the amount of economic damage done by the various taxes. Quite a lot is known about this subject as a result of panel-data studies and simulations using macroeconomic models, even if politicians rarely pay attention to this work when taking decisions to raise taxes: avoiding political unpopularity seems to be the main criterion.

The evidence suggests that the most economically injurious taxes are the direct surcharges on employment, which are widely employed in the Eurozone and broadly equivalent to employers' National Insurance contributions in Britain. Taxes on income and capital are the next most damaging because of their adverse impact on saving and capital formation. Low proportional taxes on consumption seem to do the least harm. This is why the National Pension Savings Scheme (NPSS) proposed in the recent White Paper on UK pension reform looks particularly misguided,

---

3   As a technical point it is worth noting that a poor person's rate of time discount may be higher than that of a wealthier person, if they are close to the subsistence level. To take the extreme case, a starving person's rate of time discount approaches infinity.

because the extra costs it imposes on employers seem almost custom-designed to do maximum damage to employment and the wider economy.

The following quotation from Mendoza et al. (1993: 104) describes the results of one not untypical empirical analysis of the effects of higher taxes on the economic performance of the industrialised countries:

> In particular, the effective average tax rate on capital income is negatively related to savings rates, and the consumption and labour income tax rates are negatively correlated with the number of hours worked, as predicted by neo-classical equilibrium models. Moreover, the level and trend of the rate of unemployment are positively correlated with the tax on labour income, as predicted by models of equilibrium unemployment or the 'natural rate'. These relationships are stronger in panel data tests that combine time-series and cross-sectional information, but they remain strong even for time series of several individual countries.

The terms 'discriminatory' and 'non-discriminatory' are often employed to distinguish between the more harmful and the least damaging taxes, although this is arguably an excessive simplification. In addition, it is by no means clear that increasing taxes from their present high levels in Britain, and even more in much of Continental Europe, will lead to an improvement, as distinct from deterioration, in the government's financial position once allowance has been made for the adverse 'second-round' effects of higher rates of tax on the private sector tax base and welfare payments. The situation varies to some extent, however, with the tax concerned. Responsible discussants of the fiscal options have to get involved at this level of detail, which is one reason why simulations on macroeconomic models remain the least bad way of evaluating the effects of changing tax rates on the economy.

Britain's high marginal tax rates

More generally, any worthwhile analysis of the consequences of taxes has to concentrate on incentive effects at the margin. In particular, the various measures of the ratio of taxes to GDP discussed in Chapter 2 represent an average, rather than a marginal measure, in two distinct senses: first, they do not allow for the fact that the marginal rate of tax may be far higher than the average rate in progressive tax systems; and second, they represent an average over all citizens. As far as the first point is concerned, it is instructive to compare the arithmetic change in total UK general government expenditure and non-oil tax revenues between 1996/97, the last financial year in which the Conservatives held office, and 2005/06 with the arithmetic rise in the basic-price measure of non-oil GDP over the same period. This comparison shows that some 52.25 per cent of the rise in money national output between 1996/97 and 2005/06 was absorbed in higher government spending and 47.25 per cent in increased non-oil taxes. If one takes a piggybacking bureaucrat's view of the tax base, however, and divides the increase in taxes over this period by the rise in non-oil GDP less the increase in government spending, the marginal loss of private sector output to the taxman rises to almost 99 per cent.[4] It should probably not be a surprise that the growth rate of Britain's private sector

4   In other words, for every pound of extra non-oil GDP that has been generated in the private sector by UK citizens, an almost matching 99p has been confiscated in higher taxes.

output may be slowing when the marginal rate of confiscation reaches these levels.

On the second point, there appear to be at least four classes of citizen whose tax burdens can be very different. There are the limited numbers of high-income individuals who accurately report their income to HM Revenue and Customs and carry a quite disproportionate share of the costs of the state. Second, there is the significant number of people who live off the state and either enjoy 365 tax-free days each year or have a negative tax burden if benefits are defined as negative taxes. Third, there are large numbers who both pay tax but also receive from the state through a complex structure of benefits, credits and reliefs, some of whom end up as net beneficiaries while others do not: this phenomenon is known as 'fiscal churning', and can give rise to high administrative and compliance costs as the tax and benefits system becomes more complex. Such pointless costs represent a pure loss of social utility, even if they are treated as part of general government current expenditure by the ONS and are included in the official measure of GDP. The final group that needs to be distinguished is the unknown number of people who do not report their activities to the fiscal authorities and instead work in the underground economy, although this group could overlap with the second one if there is welfare fraud.

The result of all this complexity is that the share of a typical private sector worker's marginal product that is absorbed by the state – which is what matters for incentives and the allocation of resources – is higher than the ratio of taxes to GDP would suggest. This can be true even if one only allows for the effects of income tax and National Insurance contributions (NICs) in devouring take-home pay. These mean that the typical standard-rate taxpayer was obliged to hand over 41.5 per cent of his or her marginal product to the state in the 2005/06 fiscal year, while the higher-rate taxpayer surrendered 47.7 per cent, if it is assumed that a worker's marginal product equals gross pay plus employer's NICs. This trade-off looks even worse, however, when allowance is made for the 17.5 per cent rate of VAT on expenditure financed out of net income, which implies approximate total marginal tax wedges of almost 52 per cent for the standard rate, and almost 57 per cent for the higher-rate taxpayer. Furthermore, these calculations are underestimates if anything because they ignore other indirect taxes (excise duties, council tax, etc.), which mean that over one fifth of household consumption is absorbed in all forms of indirect taxation. There is also the loss of tax credits and other benefits as incomes expand, which adds to the marginal tax cost of earning an extra pound of income for many people. The scale of the tax penalties on marginal effort, which is what matters for incentives, the expenses associated with employment (such as travel costs) and the fact that leisure is a tax-free good mean that it is not surprising that so many older male workers have dropped out of the workforce – often on to the more generous invalidity, rather than unemployment, benefit – and that so many of the more poorly educated youngsters have joined the untaxed criminal underclass.

Do high marginal rates of tax really cause disincentives?

Left-liberal economists still tend to argue that the effect of higher taxes on work effort is theoretically ambiguous, because the loss of income caused by increased taxes encourages people to work harder and this offsets the so-called substitution effect, whereby leisure was made more attractive than work effort.[5] The work of US supply-side economists, however, such as the 2004 Nobel laureate Edward Prescott, has demonstrated that the substitution effect is far more powerful in practice and that the elasticity of labour supply with respect to the post-tax real wage is probably around three, and certainly nowhere near zero. Professor Prescott was also able to use this phenomenon to explain why working hours appear to have fallen sharply in Europe over the past three decades but not in the USA (see Prescott, 2004). Prescott's research was subsequently taken further in an ECB Occasional Paper by Leiner-Killinger et al. (2005). These authors found:

> Countries with a relatively high tax wedge (which captures the amount of social security contributions, payroll taxes, personal income tax and consumer taxes that create a wedge between real labour costs for employers and the real take-home pay of employees) tend to record a lower level of annual hours worked per capita. Belgium, France, Italy and the Netherlands, for example, which were at the low end of the annual hours worked per capita scale in the euro area in 2004, have particularly high tax wedges. Countries with high marginal tax rates, for example, Belgium Germany and the Netherlands, also show some tendency towards shorter average annual hours per worker, especially among women.

---

5   In fact, even if their argument were true, it would not be relevant to wider measures of welfare. It is only so-called substitution effects caused by people reducing work effort because of high marginal tax rates which matter for measuring the dead-weight losses of taxation discussed earlier. It is strange that left-leaning economists should argue that high marginal tax rates might not matter because they do not affect work effort overall. Their argument relies on the fact that households may have to increase hours worked to make up for the income lost through taxation (the so-called income effect). It should be clear that there are no great economic or wider social benefits from households, particularly those with children, having to work longer hours simply to pay tax bills.

Reductions in labour taxes probably contributed to the increase in average annual hours worked per capita in some countries, such as Ireland, in the second half of the 1990s.

From a methodological perspective, what is impressive about such studies is their ability to account for phenomena, such as high European unemployment, that are often either taken for granted or explained in terms of sociological phenomena or crude Marxist models of exploitation. There is clearly a place for sociological and other such insights to be used to supplement the economic approach, but this should surely only be after the considerable explanatory powers of positive economics have been exhausted first.

A final comment is that the coming on-stream of new low-tax economies, such as China, may have reduced both the optimal size of the public sector in, say, western Europe and altered the desirable structure of taxation, if it is the relative rather than the absolute tax and spending burdens which determine the competitiveness of a nation's industries on world markets.[6] Under these circumstances, new low-tax competitors lower the optimal size of the state, even if the marginal benefit from government spending is unchanged, and place disproportionate pressure on the high-tax-and-spender's tradable goods sector. The latter may have to be

6   In a sense, the term competitiveness is not especially meaningful and perhaps a misuse of the economic concept of 'competition'. If the government takes a super-optimal share of GDP, economic welfare will fall and people will be poorer. Some sectors of the economy will suffer more than others. In theory the economy could still operate at a high level of employment, though combined with a lower level of economic welfare. The existence of welfare benefits means, however, that, if government spending rises, it becomes more likely that after-tax earnings will be insufficiently attractive to induce people to work. Trade with lower-tax economies will therefore cause unemployment in the tradable goods sector.

alleviated by cutting payroll taxes and raising consumer taxes, for example, which is the policy now being pursued in Germany.

One reason for the serious problems now gripping much of Europe may be that its electorate and political institutions have not realised that the generous welfare provision that was affordable when countries were competing with similar welfare-heavy societies is no longer supportable in a unified world economy where instant communications make relative production costs transparent, and just about any nation can gain access to the best production technologies going. Most analyses of the effects of government spending have tended to use a closed economy paradigm (Funke and Nickel, 2006, is an exception). The IMF has recently developed an open economy macro model for fiscal policy evaluations, however, which is starting to produce some interesting analyses (see Botman et al., 2006, and Box 6 opposite). The scale and speed of the adverse effects of high taxes appear to be amplified in an open economy framework, in part because of the international mobility of productive labour as well as of financial and physical capital from high- to low-tax economies. This is a special case of the more general situation that the effects of government spending and taxation can vary with aspects of the wider economic environment that are usually ignored in the political debate. The varying importance of these deeper influences may help explain why more conclusive results have not been obtained from cross-section and panel-data studies. The extent to which potential emigration by a highly taxed minority can limit the predatory redistributive power of the poorer majority operating through the state has recently been examined in a mathematically rigorous paper by Boerner and Uebelmesser (2005). It is also a major practical policy concern in countries such as New

Box 6 **The IMF's analysis of the fiscal consolidation options facing Britain**

The IMF used their open economy fiscal policy model to analyse the options for fiscal consolidation in the UK (see Botman and Honjo, 2006). Their conclusions are reproduced below because they differ so strikingly from the terms in which these issues are discussed by Britain's political class.

- There are significant potential benefits from early fiscal adjustment. The long-term gains of preventing a rise in government debt more than outweigh the short-term costs of fiscal adjustment.
- Reducing transfers or government spending on goods provides larger gains than raising taxes. In particular, raising corporate or personal income tax rates creates larger distortions by reducing capital accumulation.
- The benefits of early consolidation decline if consumers have a longer planning horizon, but increase if consumption is less sensitive to changes in the interest rate. These behavioural assumptions affect the crowding-out effects of government debt and therefore the costs of delaying fiscal adjustment.
- Consolidating through reducing transfers or lowering government spending becomes more attractive if workers are more sensitive to changes in the after-tax real wage. This factor increases the distortions created by raising labour income taxes, also making consolidation through raising other types of taxation relatively more attractive.
- A reduction in global savings would make early consolidation more urgent from both cyclical and long-term perspectives. A reduction in global savings increases the real interest rate in a small open economy such as the United Kingdom. This causes a substantial reduction in investment, more than offsetting any positive effects on UK exports. Higher interest rates also increase the costs of debt service substantially, requiring larger fiscal adjustments in case it is delayed.
- Tax reform aimed at increasing incentives to save could provide support to fiscal consolidation measures. This applies in particular to the long-term benefits of early fiscal adjustment.

Zealand, however, which is now suffering a substantial outward migration to Australia, where taxes are lower and have recently been reduced.

More generally, international trade is a positive-sum game, and wealthy countries arguably have a duty to poorer nations, not only to eliminate trade barriers, but also to maximise their own growth in order to provide markets for poor-country exporters. The USA seems by and large to have fulfilled this moral obligation in recent years, much to the benefit of countries such as China. In contrast, the sluggish growth of 'Old Europe' has been a major handicap to all its trading partners. This adverse effect has operated independently of the EU's protectionism, and its tendency to dump surplus agricultural production on world markets, and may have done more harm to developing countries than international aid, which European politicians like to boast about, has brought benefits. This is another illustration of the general principle that responsible people should never look at the effects of government spending in isolation but should always bear in mind the opportunity cost of the resources taken by the state to pay for it.

5   DOES BRITAIN HAVE REGIONAL JUSTICE IN TAX AND SPEND?

This chapter examines the regional aspects of government spending in the UK. Chapter 6 returns to the wider macroeconomic issues and examines the question of the optimal size of the public sector.

Regions in UK public finance

The UK has a highly centralised political system by international standards, and it is only in recent years that even partly reliable regional statistics have become available. This chapter examines a range of data for twelve UK regions. Its main finding is the striking differences between the various regions of the UK with respect to: living costs; output per capita; propensities to work; and the degree of socialisation. It concludes that imposing an onerous and interventionist tax and benefit system on a nation with such wide regional differences does significant injustice to the parts of the UK with a high marginal product in cash terms, and unduly favours cheaper and less productive areas. It also suggests that high public spending can damage local employment, even when it is provided as a 'free good' from outside. This suggestion is consistent with the evidence from the international growth literature that excessive welfare benefits are output-destroying.

Table 14 **Key demographic statistics for the UK regions**

	Population mid-2004 (000s)	Economically active in April–June 2006 (%)	Employment rate in April–June 2006 (%)	Labour Force Survey unemployment in April–June 2006 (%)	Non-white population in 2004 (%)	Households in receipt of benefits in 2003/04* (%)	Workless households in autumn 2005 (%)
North-east	2,545.1	76.4	71.7	6.1	2.9	76 (32)	21.8
North-west	6,827.2	77.5	73.3	5.2	6.0	72 (31)	17.8
Yorks & Humber	5,038.8	78.8	74.2	5.7	7.5	72 (30)	16.7
East Midlands	4,279.7	81.4	76.9	5.4	7.4	68 (30)	12.8
West Midlands	5,334.0	78.4	73.9	5.6	11.4	70 (29)	15.9
South-west	5,038.2	81.6	78.5	3.8	2.6	69 (34)	13.6
East	5,491.3	81.1	76.9	5.0	5.5	68 (31)	12.6
London	7,429.2	75.5	69.4	7.9	32.1	60 (22)	20.1
South-east	8,110.2	82.9	79.0	4.6	5.8	67 (31)	11.9
England	50,093.8	79.3	74.9	5.5	10.1	69 (30)	15.7
Scotland	5,078.4	79.3	74.8	5.5	2.3	71 (30)	18.5
Wales	2,952.5	75.9	71.4	5.7	2.3	73 (32)	18.5
Northern Ireland	1,710.3	73.4	70.2	4.2	0.9	78 (27)	19.6
UK	59,834.9	79.0	74.6	5.5	8.8	69 (30)	16.2

Sources: UK Office for National Statistics, Regional Trends 2006, and Labour Market Statistics, first release, 16 August 2006.
* Figures in brackets are retirement benefits only.

Key differences between the UK regions

Table 14 summarises the main demographic and labour-market features of the twelve main regions into which the UK is officially subdivided. There are nine government office regions in England, plus Scotland, Wales and Northern Ireland.

It is worth noting that a detailed examination of the data suggests that the differences within regions are far larger than the differences between regions. These intra-regional differences need to be borne in mind when considering the regional data presented here. A number of features emerge from Table 14. The first is the wide spread of population sizes between the various regions. Northern Ireland contains just over 1.7 million people, but south-east England has over 8 million citizens. Second, there are the strikingly different propensities to be employed, with over 9.8 percentage points more of the population of working age having jobs in the south-east than in Northern Ireland, for example. Third, there are noticeable regional differences in unemployment, as measured by the official Labour Force Survey (LFS). Fourth, there exist huge differences in the ethnic composition of the various regions, with 32.1 per cent of Londoners being non-white in 2004, but only 0.9 per cent of the Northern Irish and 2.3 per cent of the Scots and Welsh. Finally, there are noticeably different propensities to be on welfare benefits, with 'only' 36 per cent of households receiving non-retirement-related benefits in the south-east, but 41 per cent in Wales, 44 per cent in the north-east and 51 per cent in Northern Ireland.

Table 15 sets out the contribution of the various regions to UK GDP/GVA (gross value added) measured at basic prices (see Chapter 2 for details of the various GDP definitions concerned). The figures nominally refer to 2004 and are taken from Marais

(2006). There are three caveats with respect to the ONS data presented by Marais, however, and these mean that it has to be interpreted with some care. One slightly odd feature of the ONS regional statistics is that the so-called annual regional GVA figures are not genuine annual data but five-year moving averages. This means that the alleged 2004 figure is an average of the period from 2000 to 2004 and is centred on 2002, but has then been scaled up to match the cash value of UK GVA in 2004. The ONS has highlighted the five-year averages because the raw annual figures are too volatile to be relied upon, although the raw series are available from the ONS data bank. Another quirk in the ONS data is that there is an '*extra-regio*' component of GVA, which reflects activities such as North Sea energy production that cannot be allocated to specific regions, and explains why the UK total exceeds the sum of its components. The final point to be aware of is that regional incomes have been allocated on a residence basis in Table 15, and this means that the income of commuters has been allocated to where they live, rather than their place of work. Workplace-based estimates are also compiled by the ONS, however, and are presented in Marais (ibid.). In practice, the figures are identical for all regions apart from London, whose GVA rises to £185.4 billion on a workplace basis, and eastern England and the south-east, where GVA falls to £89.4 billion and £148.7 billion respectively, reflecting the well-known commuting patterns in the area concerned.

Table 15 brings out the extent to which England dominates the UK total, and the fact that London, the east and the south-east – which might be regarded as one large 'travel-to-work' area – together contribute 42.1 per cent of UK GVA, compared with Scotland's 8.2 per cent, Wales's 3.9 per cent and Northern Ireland's 2.3

Table 15 Regional gross value added (GVA) in nominal and in real terms

	GVA at current basic prices (£m in 2004)	GVA as share of UK total (%)	GVA per capita (£)	GVA per capita as indices (UK=100)	Average regional price in 2004 (UK=100)	GVA corrected for price differential (£m)	Real GVA per capita as indices (UK=100)
North-east	34,188	3.4	13,433	79.9	94.2	14,260	84.9
North-west	101,996	10.1	14,940	88.9	96.9	15,418	91.8
Yorks & Humber	75,219	7.5	14,928	88.8	94.2	15,847	94.3
East Midlands	65,770	6.5	15,368	91.5	97.4	15,778	93.9
West Midlands	81,745	8.1	15,325	91.2	97.8	15,670	93.3
South-west	78,650	7.8	15,611	92.9	101.3	15,411	91.7
East	100,307	10.0	18,267	108.7	101.1	18,068	107.5
London	164,961	16.4	22,204	132.2	109.7	20,241	120.5
South-east	158,187	15.7	19,505	116.1	105.3	18,523	110.2
England	861,022	85.6	17,188	102.3	–	–	–
Scotland	82,050	8.2	16,157	96.2	94.5	17,098	101.8
Wales	39,243	3.9	13,292	79.1	93.7	14,186	84.4
Northern Ireland	23,058	2.3	13,482	80.2	93.1	14,481	86.2
UK	1,033,324	100.0	16,802	100.0	100.0	16,802	100.0

Source: ONS (see articles cited in main text).

per cent. The third and fourth columns of Table 15 show the variations in the value of GVA per capita in cash terms, also expressed as indices. This is as far as the official statistics normally go. It is possible, however, using the data in Wingfield et al. (2005), to correct the cash GVA figures for the differences in regional living costs (including housing) observed in 2004, and this is done in the final two columns.

It is clear from these calculations that the fact that London is some 16.5 per cent more expensive than the north-east, for example, means that the simple cash figures overstate the degree of regional inequality between regional incomes and output (this is broadly the same issue as whether one should compare national GDP using market-exchange rates or purchasing power parities). The regional differences in living costs are important, because much of the justification for the transfers from one part of the UK to another appears to be based on the idea that certain places are poorer than others. If these transfers do not allow for regional differences in living costs, however, they can end up suffering from a 'money illusion', and shift resources from places that are poorer in real terms to those that are better off. Thus, in cash terms, London appears to have a GVA per head that is 65.25 per cent higher than that of the north-east, but this gap shrinks to 42 per cent once relative living costs are taken into account. Likewise, Scotland appears to have a 3.75 per cent lower GVA per head in cash terms than the UK average, but this reverses to being 1.75 per cent above the national average once relative costs are allowed for; while the Welsh shortfall drops from almost 21 to 15.5 per cent. This does not mean that the relative regional consumer price level is a perfect measure for deflating GVA, and there are serious measurement problems, including competing ways of weighting the basket of goods and services (we have used national weights), which are discussed in Wingfield et al. (2005). Even so, it is clearly better as a general principle to carry out a rough-and-ready adjustment than to make no allowance whatsoever for the wide differences in regional price levels that prevail within the UK.

Regional breakdown of public spending

British governments have been engaging in regional policies ever since the 1930s. This support has taken both overt forms, such as regional development grants, and implicit forms, such as the transfer of resources from one region to the next by means of the tax and benefit system. The HM Treasury publication *Public Expenditure: Statistical Analyses 2006* breaks down government spending by region, and it is possible to combine these figures with the regional GDP data to estimate the degree of socialisation of each part of the UK. There are a number of adjustments that have to be made to the figures before this is possible, however. This means that the data should be regarded as approximate, rather than precise.

One problem is that the regional spending figures refer to fiscal years, while the GVA statistics are smoothed calendar-year ones. We have tackled this problem by scaling the GVA figures on to a financial-year basis, using the corresponding ratios for national GVA, which is available in both forms. A second difficulty is that it is not possible to allocate all government spending on to a regional basis. What we have done here is to scale up the HM Treasury regional figures so that they sum to the equivalent national totals. In practice, this means that they have been boosted by 23.9 per cent. A third issue, already encountered in

Chapter 2, is that there are three separate ways of measuring GDP, and the chosen option can make a noticeable difference to the ratios concerned. As a result, Table 16 presents the regional public spending ratios on all three GDP bases for 2004/05, where the basic-price regional GDP estimates have been scaled up to their factor cost and market-price equivalents, using the UK ratios for the same financial year. *Public Expenditure: Statistical Analyses 2006* provides historical figures back to 2000/01 and 'plans' for 2005/06, although we decided not to use the latter because it was not yet hard data and the figures were approximate enough already.

The first thing that emerges from Table 16 is the incredible differences that can be observed between different areas of the economy, with government expenditure in south-east England amounting to only 35.8 per cent of the factor cost measure of GDP, while the equivalent figures for Scotland, Wales and Northern Ireland are 58.5, 67.9 and 75.8 per cent respectively. Indeed, the figures suggest that north-east England, Wales and Northern Ireland almost qualify as Potemkin economies, with virtually no ability to stand on their own two feet.

This acute dependency is noteworthy, given the length of time that public money has been pumped into these areas, and contrasts with the speed with which many of the liberated economies of eastern Europe have turned themselves around. The most plausible explanation for this endemic reliance on welfare is probably the supply-side argument that total hours worked are highly sensitive to the post-tax and benefit trade-off between work and leisure. A complementary political-economy explanation is that being in receipt of transfers is positively harmful, because it encourages people to look towards political activism and state

Table 16 General government expenditure in 2004/05 by country and region

	Identified public spending 2004/05 (£m)	Scaled public spending 2004/05 (£m)	Estimated GDP at basic prices in 2004/05 (£m)	Ratio to GDP at factor cost prices (%)	Ratio to GDP at basic prices (%)	Ratio to GDP at market prices (%)	Proportion employed in the public sector* (%)
North-east	18,241	22,592	34,566	66.4	65.4	58.1	23.7
North-west	47,312	58,596	103,125	57.7	56.8	50.4	21.5
Yorks & Humber	32,063	39,710	76,051	53.0	52.2	46.3	20.3
East Midlands	25,099	31,085	66,498	47.4	46.7	41.5	17.9
West Midlands	33,559	41,563	82,650	51.1	50.3	44.7	19.5
South-west	30,036	37,200	79,520	47.5	46.8	41.5	20.4
East	30,779	38,120	101,417	38.2	37.6	31.3	18.6
London	55,938	69,280	166,787	42.2	41.5	36.8	19.0
South-east	45,609	56,487	159,938	35.8	35.2	31.3	17.6
England	318,636	394,633	870,551	46.0	45.3	40.2	19.5
Scotland	38,581	47,783	82,958	58.5	57.6	51.1	23.8
Wales	21,400	26,504	39,677	67.9	66.8	59.3	23.3
Northern Ireland	14,052	17,403	23,313	75.8	74.6	66.2	29.8
UK	392,669	486,323	1,044,760	47.2	46.5	41.3	20.3

Sources: HM Treasury, ONS and author's estimates (see Smith, 2005, for further details).

* Average of four quarters to 2005 Q2. The original Labour Force Survey figures have been scaled down by the ONS (see Hicks et al., 2005, for details).

dependency for economic betterment, rather than to their own efforts in the marketplace.

A comparison of the regional UK figures with the data provided by the OECD in the annexe to its June 2006 *Economic Outlook*, which shows the ratio of general government outlays to market-price GDP for the 27 OECD member countries (Table 25, p. 187), reveals that south-east England would qualify as possessing the second-lowest public expenditure burden in the OECD after South Korea, while Wales exceeds Sweden's topside record by almost 1 percentage point and Northern Ireland overshoots it by 7.75 percentage points. It is also interesting that if London, the south-east and the east are treated as a unit, their combined government expenditure amounts to 34 per cent of market-price GDP. This is below Ireland, the USA, Switzerland and Australia, which are all usually considered to be low-tax and low-government-spending economies, and would leave the London/south-east/east bloc with the second-lowest public spending share in the OECD area, after South Korea.

It will be seen in Chapter 6 that Tanzi and Schuknecht (2000) and Tanzi (2004) have argued that there are few returns, in terms of objective measures of social welfare, such as the United Nations' Human Development Indices (HDIs), from pushing the size of the government sector much beyond 30–35 per cent of market-price GDP. The fact that the London/south-east/east bloc meets this criterion, despite recent significant rises in its spending ratio, and yet still flourishes, provides support for this view. The London/south-east/east bloc has a far higher tax burden, however, than is implied by its level of public spending, because of the transfers to other areas of the country. These outward transfers appear particularly hard on London, which has some unique problems, including in areas such as public health, where diseases such as Aids and tuberculosis are increasingly common.

Is high public spending damaging, even when provided free?

It was suggested in Chapters 3 and 4 that the main problem with pushing government spending beyond its optimal point was not that it inevitably generated zero or negative marginal social benefits, but that it had to be paid for and that all the possible methods of payment had adverse consequences, which eventually outweighed the gains and led to: slower growth; increased structural unemployment; and possible higher inflation, if the monetary authority became subservient to the politicians.

The persistent underperformance of certain areas of the UK, despite decades of massive transfers from outside, gives rise to the more disturbing possibility that high levels of government spending are themselves responsible for many of the problems of the poorer regions of the UK – even if the public spending is not financed through taxation but by transfers from other parts of the country.

This might seem paradoxical at first sight, and gives rise to the question of how large amounts of free money can possibly be harmful. One set of explanations can be found in the relatively new approach of behavioural economics (see Beaulier and Caplan, 2002, for example), but there are also good reasons in the more traditional economics of labour markets that explain why such transfers can be a problem.

Most economic textbooks have a diagram such as Figure 12, which shows the marginal product of labour and the cost of

Figure 12 **How government-imposed costs destroy jobs**

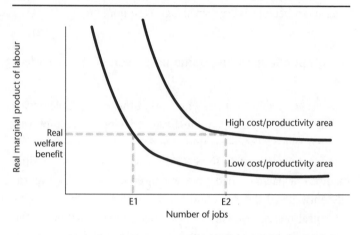

employing labour on the vertical axis, and a curve that slopes downwards to the right relating the two. The chart can then be used to show why introducing a mandatory minimum wage, paying benefits to people who do not want to work, or imposing high levels of social overhead costs, such as employer's National Insurance contributions, can cause the employment of the least productive workers to be truncated. This is because it either costs more to employ them than they are worth, or because potential employees would rather draw benefits (this benefit rate, minimum wage or social overhead cost appears as a horizontal line in the diagram below: if productivity is below the benefit rate employment will not take place). There is considerable debate with respect to the scale of these effects, but few economists would deny the logic of this argument.

Such textbook diagrams are usually taken to refer to the

economy as a whole. If, however, there is a series of distinct regional labour markets, with imperfect mobility between them, there will not be one such curve but many, with the high-productivity/high-cost-of-living areas having curves well above those of the poorer and less productive regions. Imposing one national minimum wage or level of unemployment benefit, in cash terms, will correspondingly have quite different employment-destroying effects in different areas of the country. For example, employment in a low-productivity area, such as the north-east of England, will settle at E_1, representing fewer jobs than in a high-productivity area such as the south-east (E_2), even if both areas have the same *absolute* level of welfare benefits or minimum wage, etc. Because welfare benefits (and the minimum wage) are the same in cash terms throughout the UK, they have greater adverse effects on employment in the low-productivity areas as measured in current prices. The 'free money' that finances welfare benefits in Northern Ireland, Wales, Scotland and northern England through taxes collected in London and the south-east actually diminishes employment in the former regions due to its microeconomic effects.

This effect seems to be what has happened in the UK, and was also the situation in East Germany, where West German employment costs were imposed on an economy where output per head was only around one third of that in the west. A trans-atlantic example of the same adverse processes at work can be found in Puerto Rico, where the availability of US levels of social support seems to have destroyed what at one point looked like a prospective economic miracle (see Economist, 2006).

One palliative would be to introduce regional differentials in welfare benefits, to reflect the divergent productivity and living costs of the regions concerned, and the present government once toyed with a similar idea with respect to public sector pay. Another approach, widely practised in nations with a federal structure, is to make welfare benefits a responsibility of devolved arms of government, such as states, provinces or cantons. Historically, in Britain, much welfare was provided at the parish level, which meant that the beneficiary and the administrator often knew each other well, something that tended to be more helpful to the 'deserving poor' who had been rendered destitute by genuine misfortune than the 'undeserving poor'. The local administration of welfare allows benefits to be set more appropriately to local conditions, and can reduce the problems caused by setting one benefit level across a heterogeneous area. It also explains why social harmonisation at the European Union level would be a potential disaster, since almost no one would bother to work in Portugal, southern Italy or Greece if they could access Swedish or German levels of unemployment benefit. It is an interesting thought experiment, however, to consider what would happen to German unemployment, or the number of Dutch sickness benefit claimants – which contains a remarkably large proportion of young males with alleged depression – if benefits in these countries were harmonised at Portuguese levels.

Regional justice, or regional injustice, in tax and spend

A fair tax system should levy the same real burden on people with the same real income, and should not take a larger share of, say, a plumber's real wages in London than it does in Newcastle, simply because the cost of living is dearer in the former than in the latter. Likewise, the allocation of government spending should be based on providing citizens who have the same physical needs with the same volume of public services, regardless of whether the services cost more to provide in one location than another. Otherwise, the distributional effects of what is now a highly interventionist state become arbitrary and unjustifiable, as is arguably now the case in Britain. The situation is likely to get worse as the scale of government spending and other interventions continues to rise.

Table 17 shows the reported level of government spending on a per capita basis (not scaled up, unlike Table 16) in cash terms, and also after correction for regional variations in the cost of living. It can be seen that the south-east and the east get a raw deal, even in nominal terms. This becomes more noticeable in real terms, however, while the relatively privileged positions of the Celtic fringe and the north-east become more apparent. One example is that per capita expenditure in Northern Ireland is 46 per cent higher than in the south-east in nominal terms, but 65.25 per cent higher in real terms.

Unfortunately, there are no definitive figures for the tax receipts generated by the various parts of the UK, although MacSearraigh et al. (2006) do provide some interesting figures for the partial concept of current taxes, which show the per capita current taxes paid by inner Londoners running some 60–80 per cent above the UK average over the past decade, while at the other extreme the inhabitants of Cornwall and the Isles of Scilly have paid some 36 per cent less per capita in recent years. The next two columns of Table 17 attempt further understanding of this phenomenon by adjusting the starting points for income tax, and the higher-rate threshold, for the difference in nominal GVA per employee in each region. This is being used as a proxy for the mean point of the earnings distribution. The next column adjusts the inheritance tax (IHT) threshold to take account of regional differences in house prices at the start of the 2005/06 financial year. Clearly, estates contain assets other than houses, but homes appear to be the dominant asset in the case of small estates, where inheritance tax first starts to bite. It is notable that people in London face house prices 2.1 times higher than those in Scotland, for example, and that the starting point for higher-rate income tax should be around £12,954 higher in London than in Northern Ireland, if people at the same point in their regional income distributions were to be taxed equivalently.

Regional conclusions

The main conclusion from this chapter is the striking variations between the different parts of the UK. The main policy implication is that imposing an onerous and interventionist tax and benefit system on a nation with such wide regional differences does substantial injustice to the parts of the country with a high cost of living and a high output per head, and unduly benefits the cheaper and less productive areas. The failure of large parts of the UK to prosper, however, despite the fact that their public spending comes as a free good from outside the region, suggests that high public spending, like excessive consumption of free alcohol, can be directly harmful in itself. Thus both donor and recipient appear to be damaged by this enforced redistribution. Employment is probably reduced by regional transfers because nationally set benefit scales, and interventions such as the minimum wage, price more people out of work in the cheaper and less productive areas of the country, and engender a 'dole culture', if sustained over several generations. This 'pricing out' may also explain the differ-

Box 7 The effects of devolution

The figures quoted in Chapter 5 are 'top-down' ones, produced by the ONS. The devolved assemblies in Scotland and Wales, however, mean that information can be obtained 'bottom up' from the websites of the assemblies concerned. This information is more extensive in the case of Scotland because of its size and the greater powers that have been devolved to the Scottish Parliament. One reason why Scotland and Wales are of interest is that they provide controlled experiments, which demonstrate the social gains or losses that occur when public spending is higher than the UK average. The publication *Government Expenditure & Revenue in Scotland*, which is laid before the Scottish Parliament, provides rich detail on the disturbing fiscal situation in that country. Unfortunately, devolution has led to a Balkanisation of nationwide statistics, and data collected for the devolved assemblies can differ from the ONS statistic for the same item, although attempts are now being made to reconcile the figures. This is another example of the problems that bedevil attempts to get a hard statistical grip on what is happening in the public sector. The two most important Scottish websites are www.scotland.gov.uk and www.scottish.parliament.uk, while information on Wales can be found on www.wales.gov.uk.

ences in joblessness between superficially similar ethnic groups, which are far too wide to be explained by racial prejudice.

The fact that London, the south-east and east England together account for almost 42 per cent of UK GDP, and have a combined government spending burden of only 34 per cent of the market-price measure of GDP, is consistent with the views of economists, described later on in Chapter 6, who have argued that there are almost no welfare gains from pushing government expenditure beyond the 30–35 per cent mark. Unfortunately, one can only dream about how much wealth could potentially have been generated for the country as a whole if these areas had not been used as milk cows to support cheaper and less productive regions in semi-permanent quasi-idleness.[1] Money is not everything, of course, and it can be argued that the real concern is the moral-hazard effects of the present intrusive and arbitrary system of welfare payments on what the Victorians would have called the 'moral character' of the recipients.

A final and sobering conclusion is that the increased complexity and extent of the tax burden since 1997 mean that the UK tax system may have become so unjust between the different regions that it is indefensible, and risks stimulating political forces that eventually lead to a break-up of the UK. The rise of the Northern League in Italy, and of secessionist sentiment in Catalonia in Spain, shows what can happen when the more economically advanced parts of a nation feel that they are being unduly exploited to benefit other regions. Similar tensions contributed to the 'velvet divorce' between the Czechs and Slovaks, and appear to rear their heads wherever there are cultural, linguistic, ethnic or religious differences between groups of citizens. This is arguably now the case in Britain, where the ethnic composition of London, for example, is very different from that of Wales or Scotland.

---

1   No criticism of the recipients of this largesse is necessarily intended by the term 'idleness'. Those who are unemployed as a result of such regional policies are the victims of economic policies that fail to take account of human nature and the impact of economic incentives on behaviour, including that of potential employers in the private sector.

Table 17 **Public expenditure per capita and tax thresholds adjusted for relative regional incomes and house prices**

	Public spending per capita in 2004/05 (£)	Price-deflated public spending (£)	Personal allowance for income tax (£)	Starting point for 40% income tax (£)	IHT threshold corrected for house prices (£)	Regional house prices in March 2006	Gross value added per filled job (UK=100)
North-east	7,167	7,608	4,642	30,703	199,226	135,125	92.2
North-west	6,930	7,152	4,602	30,436	218,219	148,007	91.4
Yorks & Humber	6,363	6,755	4,542	30,037	217,828	147,742	90.2
East Midlands	5,865	6,022	4,909	32,468	234,437	159,007	97.5
West Midlands	6,291	6,433	4,763	31,502	242,997	164,813	94.6
South-west	5,962	5,885	4,672	30,902	297,251	201,611	92.8
East	5,605	5,544	5,080	33,600	302,917	205,454	100.9
London	7,530	6,864	6,279	41,525	404,147	274,113	124.7
South-east	5,624	5,341	5,246	34,699	343,708	233,120	104.2
England	6,361	–	5,100	33,733	287,506	195,001	101.3
Scotland	7,597	8,039	4,874	32,234	195,018	132,271	96.8
Wales	7,248	7,735	4,516	29,870	219,267	148,718	89.7
Northern Ireland	8,216	8,825	4,320	28,571	208,628	141,502	85.8
UK	6,563	6,563	5,035	33,300	275,000	186,519	100.0

Source: ONS and Department of Communities and Local Government (2006).

The Labour Party was not the leading party in terms of votes in England in the 2005 general election, and the 2006 local authority elections showed a clear voting divide between the regions that lived off the state and those that paid for it.

6 WHAT IS THE OPTIMAL SIZE OF THE PUBLIC SECTOR?

This chapter examines the optimal share of government spending in GDP, and considers why public spending has apparently expanded far beyond this point in many countries.

How the optimal size is less than the maximum tax take

In theory, the public sector could absorb anything from 0 per cent of GDP in a state of nature to 100 per cent in a fully planned Marxist economy. Even Soviet Russia, however, had an underground black market economy equal to around one quarter of GDP in the 1970s, while the smallest public sector recorded in Table 1 is the 5.75 per cent recorded in Sweden in 1870. This suggests that the practical limits to the size of public spending in market-price GDP are somewhere between one tenth and three-quarters, subject to all the practical measurement problems involved. This represents a massive range, however, which gives rise to the question of whether it is possible for economists to calculate the optimal size of the public sector.

There seems to be general acceptance that there are high marginal returns to increased public spending when it is starting from a low base, with the provision of the rule of law, public health measures and elementary education all boosting growth, as well as being desirable in themselves, even if there may be scope for private or mixed public/private provision in certain areas. The experience of the South-East Asian 'tiger' economies, however, suggests that such gains can be achieved with government spending no higher than 20 per cent of market-price GDP, compared with the 47.75 per cent ratio observed in the Eurozone in 2005, for example. The evidence suggests that less than one fifth of public spending in the OECD area is on growth-enhancing items, while the payment of welfare benefits to people of working age has a negative effect on growth.

Such considerations suggest that, if one plots real GDP or utility on the vertical axis and the share of government spending in GDP on the horizontal one, the result is an inverted U-shaped line, similar to the famous 'Laffer curve' (Figure 13). It would be a neat result if the revenue-maximising point on the Laffer curve coincided with the utility-maximising point on the government spending curve. There appears to be no reason, however, why they should coincide. Instead, the revenue-maximising point seems to be farther to the right, from the viewer's perspective, than the utility-maximising one (Figure 10 again). In other words, the optimal size of state from the viewpoint of public welfare may well be some 15–25 percentage points less than the maximum possible revenue that an oppressive government can extort from society.

The most significant and persistent attempts to estimate the optimal size of the state have been carried out by Tanzi and Schuknecht (1995, 2000), either jointly or individually (Tanzi, 2004). It is worth quoting the conclusion they drew as long ago as 1995 from their examination of a wide range of indicators of social well-being, for developed and newly industrialising countries, over a long period of time:

In summary, we conclude that social indicators improved the most between 1870 and 1960 when the welfare state was still in its infancy. The expansion of public expenditure and of the welfare state during the last three decades has yielded limited gains in terms of social objectives while possibly damaging the countries' economic performance. Today, countries with small governments and the newly industrialised countries show similar levels of social indicators but these are achieved with lower expenditure, lower taxes and higher growth than countries with big governments. (Tanzi and Schuknecht, 1995: 25)

Tanzi and Schuknecht then state later on in the same paper:

However, we have argued that most of the important social and economic gains can be achieved with a drastically lower level of public spending than prevails today. Perhaps, the level of public spending does not need to be much higher than 30% of GDP to achieve most of the important social and political objectives that justify governmental interventions. However, this would require radical reforms, a well-working private market, and an efficient regulatory role for the government. (ibid.: 34)

In their more recent research the authors have used objective measures of welfare, such as the United Nations' Human Development Indices (HDIs), to quantify the marginal gains from increased public spending, and have also tended to quote 30–35 per cent as the optimal range, given the uncertainties associated with the data, and these are the figures that have been used in the present monograph. The rules of thumb that appear to emerge at this point are that:

- A geopolitically ambitious society, such as China, that wished to maximise its economic growth and international power should confine government spending to below 20 per cent of market-price GDP.
- A strategically secure society – for example, the USA – that wanted to maximise economic welfare should probably expand government expenditure to no more than 35 per cent of market-price GDP, provided that the social rate of time discount is high enough to offset the slower growth than under the first option.
- Predatory politicians who wished to maximise the resources and powers of patronage under their command in the short term, and were indifferent to the long-term welfare of their populations, might push the public spending share up to the 45–50 per cent of market-price GDP that is now widespread across Europe.
- Only the seriously misguided, or a megalomaniac, would attempt to push the public spending share beyond 55 per cent. One reason is that social cohesion tends to break down in heavily socialised nations, because it becomes economically rational for everybody to try to 'plunder' the public purse in order to better themselves rather than rely on their own efforts in the marketplace.

Higher government spending ... more poverty

The conclusion at this point is that, with the possible exception of the USA, South Korea, Australia and Ireland, the state is now widely absorbing some tenth to a quarter more of national output in the developed Western economies than appears to be optimal,

Figure 13 **The effect of public spending on economic welfare (top) and the 'Laffer' curve (bottom)**

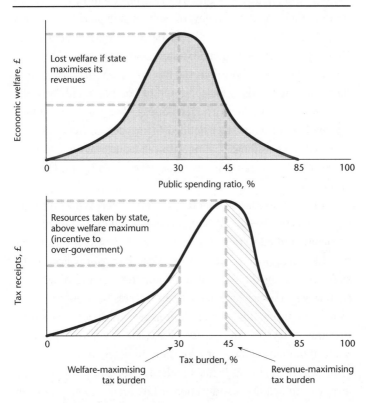

while there has been little to show for it in terms of measures of well-being, and the cost in terms of economic growth forgone has been considerable. It is highly likely that societies are poorer than they would have been if low spending ratios had been maintained. Paradoxically, this also means that there are fewer resources in

143

absolute terms available to help the needy through government redistribution in a society that tries to achieve a more even distribution of income through government spending. This point was forcibly made from a Swedish perspective by Bergström and Gidehag (2004), who demonstrated that even poor people in the USA were better off than the typical citizen of Sweden, and that living standards in Europe could be compared only with the poorest states in America's Deep South. The think tank Open Europe has subsequently extended their research by publishing a collection of readings dealing with the failures of the European social model in a range of countries (see Mullally and O'Brien, 2006).

This finding that economic growth is a necessary precondition of effective welfare provision is highly relevant to the debate on health and education, because richer societies tend to be far healthier than poorer ones for any given level of medical provision, something that was brutally apparent in the nineteenth century when better food and housing, access to clean water and proper sanitation did far more to improve life expectancies than the efforts of Victorian doctors. Likewise, the returns on investment in human capital – or education, in other words – become progressively higher as living standards rise, giving people more incentive to acquire an education, while high marginal rates of income tax reduce the net present value of participating in education, particularly if means-tested benefits then reduce the costs of the low skill base associated with not becoming educated. Such considerations mean that, even if the state had no other objectives, maximising the net present value of the health of the population, or its educational attainments, involves exactly the same trade-off between opting for a smaller state now and having higher economic growth, on the one hand, and trying to do as much as possible for today's generation at the cost of future prosperity, on the other. The same applies to many environmental concerns, where rich countries can afford to maintain better standards than poor ones, and the former communist states were infamous for the environmental damage they caused (see Lomborg, 2003, for a cool-headed appraisal of the claims of environmentalists).

If government is so bad, why do we have so much of it?

The obvious question at this point is why representative democracies have allowed so much harm to be done for so little return in terms of social welfare. To a liberal-market economist, such a non-optimal outcome must ultimately reflect the political equivalent of a market imperfection. It is conceivable that this imperfection in the political marketplace simply reflects the veniality of the political class and the gullibility of electorates, which means that they do not vote in their own best interests, although this would be hard to reconcile with the concept of rational economic behaviour.

A more systematic explanation is that too-high government spending has resulted from the breakdown in the relationship between taxation and representation, on the one hand, and representation and taxation, on the other. A simple theory of democracy can start from the assumption that the electorate behaves like a club, in which each member pays an equal subscription[1] and each has an equal voice. This model breaks down if the democratic system itself can be used to redistribute income from one group

---

1   i.e. a poll tax.

of voters to another. Once that process has taken place a large proportion of the electorate can pay nothing towards the costs of the state, but can vote for others to hand over money for their benefit, while a minority of the electorate pays a quite dispropor-tionate share of the costs of the state.[2]

A lynch mob is a perfect example of untrammelled democracy in action, because everyone apart from the victim would freely vote for the hanging. A lynching also represents a gross abuse of the human rights of the victim, however, and is indefensible on moral grounds. Unfortunately, the fiscal equivalent of this 'lynch mob' model of democracy – which can be defined as a situation in which a majority of the electorate vote to impose the burden of paying for public expenditure on to a minority off whom they intend to free-ride – now appears to be the situation in Britain, as the size of the retired, welfare-dependent and public employment rolls, compared with private sector employees, will confirm.

Currently, only just over 20 million people out of the 44.4 million on the parliamentary electoral register are employed in the private sector of the economy or are self-employed, while 7.1 million state that they work for government, 11.8 million are pensioners, 2.7 million are claiming incapacity benefit, and a large part of the residual 3.2 million (including 0.78 million lone parents) are dependent on the various other types of welfare benefit (Shaw and Sibieta, 2005, give an exhaustive tabular listing of the numbers claiming various benefits in Table 2.1 on page 5 of their study, but one has to bear in mind that one person can legitimately claim several benefits). More generally, a quick look at the global political scene since the 1950s suggests the hypothesis

---

2   See the literature on public choice economics.

that low-tax, pro-wealth-creation parties can frequently gain office when the state absorbs under 35 per cent or so of market-price GDP, but that high-tax redistributive parties appear to become entrenched once the government spending ratio is over 45 per cent, because the vested interests gaining their income from the state become a majority of the electorate.[3]

This second possibility has been described in the public choice literature, and it can lead to all political parties being drawn to a position of supporting high government spending but low-growth policies because all parties fear that they will be unable to gain a parliamentary majority if they try to stabilise or reverse the upward trend in government spending.[4] This view may be mistaken if the adverse second-round effects of high spending on economic performance are so bad that they lead to a backlash against tax-and-spend policies, however. Sometimes, specific events, such as a run on the currency or a collapse in the bond market, have also led to abrupt U-turns away from fiscal profligacy, such as the one performed by the Labour government following the 1976 IMF loan. In addition, brave statesmen and women, such as Ronald

---

3 This does not mean that such high-spending nirvanas are sustainable, however, because the resulting poor economic performance either: a) eventually leads to an economic crisis that forces a change of course; or b) lower-spending economies outgrow the high spenders to the point where the low spenders come to dominate the high spenders geopolitically and militarily, and have often proceeded to conquer them in the past (see Kennedy, 1989, for a detailed historic account of the rise and fall of the great powers). One reason for this is that demographic factors should be treated as endogenous in a properly specified model of the rise and fall of nations, and high-tax stagnant economies tend to experience low birth rates, ageing populations and outward migration, something that is now very apparent in western Europe.

4 There are many implicit and explicit references to public choice economics in the remainder of this chapter and the next chapter. A standard text is that by Mueller (2003). A good summary of the ideas appears in Tullock et al. (2000).

Reagan and Margaret Thatcher, demonstrated that it was possible to tackle the spending lobbies full-on through the force of their arguments and still gain office. It is, however, hard to see their moral and intellectual equivalents among contemporary British politicians. Furthermore, Gordon Brown's significant increase in the size of the state has created vested interests that will try to prevent a reversal of his policies, despite their potential adverse effects on economic growth and welfare and perhaps even the nation's ability to defend itself in an increasingly dangerous world.

7 NEW LABOUR, OR OLD FASCISTS?

Chapter 1 suggested that there were apparent similarities between the more interventionist elements of the Continental European and New Labour approaches and the economic systems of the pre-war fascists. These issues are investigated further here. It must be emphasised, however, that this concern is solely to do with the question of economic systems, not the poisonous racial ideology so important to the German Nazis, and it is not being suggested that fascist precedents have been consciously followed. The section 'Gathering clouds' discusses the looming fiscal problems facing Britain, while the unduly neglected interface between fiscal and monetary policy is discussed in the annexe.

Springtime for Hitler?

A simple taxonomy of economic types suggests that pure free-market capitalism of the sort that came close to prevailing in Britain in the nineteenth century, when the state absorbed at one point well under a tenth of national output, can be regarded as a system in which the owners of human, physical and financial capital can do what they like with their resources and are free to allocate the returns from their enterprise and endeavours as they see fit. Pure socialism is a system in which all the means of production are expropriated and controlled by the state, and the government decides how the resulting output is allocated between the consumption of individuals, capital formation and its own direct expenditure. A 'Butskellite' mixed economy, such as that which existed in Britain in the 1950s, is one in which the ownership of capital and the production process are generally left to market forces but a proportion of the ensuing output is creamed off – preferably in the form of non-distortionary flat-rate taxes – to support wider social goals.[1] It is also worth noting that the share of British government spending in national output was very close to Tanzi and Schuknecht's optimum in the 1950s – incidentally, the same appears to have been true of many other Western economies at the time (Table 1) – despite Britain's massive expenditure on defence by contemporary standards.

New Labour's so-called 'third way', and the prevalent economic paradigm in much of 'Old Europe', appears to correspond to none of these categories. Instead, it appears to be a system under which the private sector maintains a nominal legal control over its capital and labour, but the returns on these factors of production are so heavily influenced by tax and regulation that the public sector ends up effectively controlling such returns. This sham form of mixed economy, which needs to be distinguished from the British mixed economy of the 1950s, has traditionally been associated with fascist regimes – for example, the *gelenkte Wirtschaft* (supple or 'joined-up' economy) that Goering implemented in Nazi Germany in 1936. Such systems represent an obvious intellectual attempt to reconcile a socialist-inspired desire

---

1   Though there was a significant nationalised industry sector too. The term But-
     skellite was a pun on the names of the paternalist Conservative Chancellor of
     the Exchequer, 'Rab' Butler, and the right-of-centre Labour Party leader Hugh
     Gaitskell, and was coined to reflect the perceived consensus on economic policy
     at the time.

for a powerful interventionist state with the wealth-creating force of 'bourgeois-liberal capitalism', and tend to be popular with politicians and bureaucrats, because they force all sectors of society to kowtow to the state and its functionaries if they are to remain in business. This means that such 'third way' systems can easily generate a rich harvest of corrupt favours, and maximise the opportunities for the political and bureaucratic class to acquire plunder and reward their supporters, and seems to explain why politicians who can slip free of democratic control tend to independently rediscover and gravitate towards the fascist model of economic organisation. It is certainly not being suggested that New Labour economic policy is consciously modelled on pre-war fascist precedents but rather that a combination of the Marxist-inspired New Left ideas of the former student radicals of the 1960s and 1970s, who now compose so much of the Labour Party establishment, when combined with an intense nanny-style authoritarianism, and the practical need to get elected, produced a synthesis that ended up with an economic approach that was functionally hard to distinguish from that of fascism.

'Third way' economies also seem capable of generating rapid growth in their early years, when their burgeoning public spending components are boosting GDP, regardless of whether this is on militarism or welfare. Such economies eventually start to seize up, however, for two main reasons. The first is that investors and entrepreneurs become aware that regulatory and tax changes that affect their private returns are expropriating their capital and thus they cease to invest or take risks. This is now a serious danger with some of the regulated utilities in the UK, as well as North Sea oil producers, and might also explain Britain's relatively poor stock market performance since May 1997 (see Littlewood, 2004).

Second, regulations and controls create inefficiencies, which in turn lead to more regulation and control, until the whole system jams up to the point at which deregulation becomes essential if the system is to survive. The costs of the earlier excessive controls can then be assessed *ex post* by the rebound in output that followed their removal.

This effect can be seen from the boost to German war production that followed Speer's panic deregulation of the German economy in 1944, for example, and the success of the liberating reforms introduced by Ludwig Erhard in 1948. These scrapped virtually overnight the rigid system of controls that had been imposed on the western zone of occupation by the US, French and British military authorities and paved the way for Germany's *Wirtschaftswunder* of the 1950s. Bold 'big bang' reforms are normally undertaken only following a crisis, however, such as the one that brought Lady Thatcher to power in the 1970s. More recent examples have to be sought in the former communist countries of eastern Europe (see Balcerowicz, 2002, for example).

'New Conservatives', old Tories?

Unfortunately, the Cameron-led British Conservative Party, like Continental conservative parties such as the Christian Democratic Union (CDU) in Germany, appears to have no stomach for the bold reforms that would transform the supply side of their economies. Of course, this would not have surprised Hayek, who regarded conservatives as being unduly prone to appeasement where the increasing socialisation of society was concerned.

American commentators sometimes distinguish between 'wealth conservators', or 'Ivy League' conservatives – the equivalent

British background would be Eton and Trinity, Cambridge, or Christchurch, Oxford – who inherit wealth and are mainly concerned with avoiding measures that might endanger their position at the pinnacle of society, and the classical liberal 'wealth creators', who expect to start from nothing and want the minimum number of state-imposed obstacles to be put in their way. The self-made Victorian railway magnate George Stephenson, who started life as a miner, would be an archetypal example of the latter. This distinction helps explain why the bourgeois interest is often split when it comes to confronting the increased socialisation of many Western economies, although an equally important reason may be the extent to which middle-class people with good academic qualifications and inherited social networks find that the state provides a more comfortable living than a private sector that is exposed to the full force of global competition. There is plenty of evidence from the laboratory of life, however, ranging from the *Reformstau* gripping Continental Europe to the adverse effects of India's 'licence Raj' on the subcontinent's growth rate, to suggest that interventionist policies strangle growth and destroy the life chances of poor people. As a result, conservative wealth conservators appear to be no more than a narrow sectional grouping, whose main objective is to stifle competition arising from more dynamic social groups, including immigrants. The wealth conservators' interests certainly do not coincide with those of the ambitious and hard-working 'honest poor', including most ethnic minorities, who are precisely the people who benefit most from the opportunities for self-improvement engendered by a dynamic society.

This analysis has now strayed some way from traditional economics but it is relevant because it provides some insight into

Box 8 **The economics of happiness**

Throughout this monograph it has been assumed that economic growth is important because it raises the quantity and quality of goods and services consumed. The assumption is that high living standards are by and large a good thing, despite the obvious issues with externalities such as pollution, etc., and that increased consumption makes people happier. This conventional view has been challenged, to some extent, by the recent development of the economics of happiness. This combines the techniques typically used by economists with those more commonly used by psychologists (see Graham, 2005). One preferred technique is to use opinion poll techniques in which people are asked to describe how happy they are, and then to try to explain the general level of happiness using socio-demographic and socio-economic variables. One result of this research was the finding that, while being relatively well off appeared to make people happier, absolute wealth seemed to make little difference in the sense that richer countries appeared to be no happier than poorer ones. This finding has led some economists working in this area to suggest that economic growth does not increase happiness, and that there is a strong case for redistributive policies because it is relative incomes which matter for well-being, not absolute ones. These ideas are clearly not consistent with the main thrust of this monograph. Other findings of the happiness literature, however, such as the value people place on liberty, are.

A personal view is that the happiness literature is intellectually interesting but it is at too early a stage of development to have useful policy implications. The happiness literature also seems to break the long-established rule in welfare economics that analysis breaks down if you have to make some people worse off in order to improve the lot of others (technically happiness studies assume interdependent utility functions). Some approaches, for example, seem to assume that envy should be pandered to, the argument being that unequal income distributions cause the relative poor unhappiness, so it maximises happiness if the state confiscates the wealth of the relatively rich. It is worth noting that this would go against much religious teaching – such as the Tenth Commandment, for example – which states that you should rejoice in your neighbour's good fortune and feel happier because of it.

A more disturbing concern is that the promotion of happiness opens up a Pandora's box of possible government interventions, and could easily be used to justify the most extreme dictatorships, such as that of Stalin or Kim Il Sung. There is a parallel here with the way poverty has been redefined as relative rather than absolute poverty by the spending lobbies. If the real aim is to maximise the power of the state, then pursuing an unobtainable but attractive-sounding objective is one way to do it. The reasons some happiness research supports the line taken in this monograph is that people appear to be less concerned about income inequality in dynamic societies where self-improvement is possible than in static ones where people feel trapped in poverty, while individuals also seem happier when they have more freedom, lower taxes and less regulation, because this gives them more control over their lives. A more general issue is that the happiness approach may be philosophically misguided, because it is committing the error of 'reification' and treating an abstract concept as if it were a measurable physical object. There are disturbing parallels here with the way in which IQ tests have been misused by social engineers in the past (Gould, 1981). The famous comment by Queen Elizabeth I, made with respect to the religious disputes of her day, that she did not intend to 'make windows into men's souls', might also be applied to some of the more intrusive endeavours in this area.

the sectional interests that help entrench the status quo in countries with high government spending. Such political matters are relevant to understanding the forces at work in public choice economics.

It is also worth straying into these political areas because, as Milton Friedman once remarked, liberal-market capitalism is the best guarantor of personal liberty. It is certainly arguable that New Labour's micro-management of the economy has become a potential threat to personal freedoms, as have a number of other features of recent policy, such as Labour's constitutional 'reforms', which have removed checks and balances on the executive arm of government; the politicisation of government information since 1997; and the government's cavalier attitude to long-established civil rights (see Major, 2003, for a former prime minister's view on these issues).

Gathering clouds

The author was an economic forecaster for over three decades, and does not intend to make detailed projections for the British economy and its public finances here. The rapid expansion in the size of the state in recent years, however, means that the pressures on the public finances are patently rising, and whoever is Chancellor of the Exchequer in a few years' time will need to make unpopular decisions with respect to public expenditure as well as taxes. This prospect seems already to have been foreshadowed in both the 2005 *Pre-Budget Report* and the March 2006 Budget, which were able to make their sums add up only by positing a marked slowdown in the projected growth of real government spending in the later years of the forecast period, as well as assuming controversially high figures for the increase in national output and the tax take from any given level of GDP.

It is not just the rise in the UK tax and spending burdens to well past their optimum of 30–35 per cent of market-price GDP in recent years which is potentially damaging to the UK's economic dynamism and the country's ability to generate 'real' jobs, however, but also the detailed way in which this increase has been carried out. Recent government policy seems to ignore everything that is known about the good, and bad, buys in taxation (see above) – an issue on which there should be political consensus because any given politically determined level of government expenditure should always be financed in the least harmful way. The needless damage done to the British economy is a consequence of New Labour's reliance on raising stealthy but 'distortionary' taxes, such as employers' National Insurance contributions, and income and savings taxes, which have reduced potential economic growth by more than a flat-rate consumption tax would have done. Likewise, the available evidence suggests that most of the increased government spending has been on categories that have little positive impact on economic growth, while the massive increase in means-tested benefits is likely to retard the expansion of national output. Means-tested in-work benefits also have seriously adverse 'moral-hazard' implications for their recipients, who might otherwise be trying to improve themselves through working longer hours, studying in their own time or taking on greater responsibility at work. It also seems to be the case that increases in the government spending and tax burdens find their counterpart in an almost one-for-one reduction in the private investment ratio. This is important if new technology comes in with private capital formation, as endogenous growth theory suggests. New Labour's economically perverse spending and taxation policies are not random aberrations, however, but can be explained by public choice economics. Taxes have been deliberately made opaque and spending concentrated on groups that then have an incentive to promote the continuation of the same polices through their voting behaviour.

How not to cut the emerging deficit

At this point, it is also necessary to issue a strong warning against the naive view that attempting to raise the *ex ante* tax burden by, say, £10 billion will simply cut public borrowing by £10 billion, *ex post*. There is long-established evidence from econometric model simulations that it is necessary to raise taxes *ex ante* by a significant multiple of some two to three times the intended reduction in public borrowing *ex post*, even in the short term. This is because of the harmful second-round effects of higher taxes in reducing the tax base of private sector activity and the increased welfare payments that come with higher joblessness. There is also evidence that higher taxes lead to greater public borrowing, not a stronger fiscal position, if one looks at the consequences a few years out, when people have had a chance to fully adjust their work/leisure trade-off to the new structure of incentives, and human and physical capital have left the country. While the precise situation seems to vary significantly from one tax to another, it is by no means clear overall that future Chancellors will be capable of taxing themselves out of the hole in the public finances created by the spending policies of recent years. This concern is fully supported by the fiscal stabilisation literature.

Conclusions

The conclusions of this chapter do not make pleasant reading. The present level of government spending in Britain now appears to be well above its socially optimal level and is heading towards the maximum level of taxation that can be extracted from the public by a predatory state. The expansion of government payrolls and other forms of state dependency also means that there are strong political-economy pressures to maintain the level of public spending well above its optimal level. This makes it difficult for timid politicians, with limited moral fibre, to even contemplate fighting on a platform of higher growth and lower taxes. The specific forms of government spending and taxation that have been pursued in the last ten years have been disproportionately damaging to economic welfare, and have entrenched interest groups that have an incentive to vote for high public spending. The most likely outcome is that an attempt will be made to resolve the problems of the looming budget deficit by raising taxes. The fiscal stabilisation literature suggests, however, that this is likely to make the deficit worse, not better, as Gordon Brown found when he raised National Insurance contributions. With this in mind, it is important that the fundamental economics discussed in this monograph are widely understood by the electorate at large. The policy conclusions set out in the next chapter are unlikely to be accepted by self-serving and myopic politicians whose main goal is to achieve election by building coalitions of interest groups.

Annexe: The interface of fiscal and monetary policy

Little has been said so far about the interface between fiscal and monetary policy, despite the fact that this is an important and unduly neglected area of policy-making. One reason for this neglect is that the modern Conventional Theoretical Macroeconomic Model (CTMM) treats fiscal and monetary policy as being independent of each other. Another is that the granting of operational independence to the Bank of England, and the removal of its responsibilities for the gilt-edged market, means that fiscal and monetary policy are now institutionally separated. It is correspondingly tempting – but wrong – to believe that the MPC can ignore the government's spending plans, provided that either they are tax financed or budget deficits are funded in a responsible manner.

One reason why the monetary authorities cannot ignore tax and spending is that the measure of the output gap embodied in the usual form of the CTMM incorrectly assumes that aggregate supply is unaffected by the incentives, or lack of them, faced by private sector producers. Once the possibility of a tax-induced supply withdrawal is acknowledged, it becomes clear that the MPC has to pursue a tighter monetary policy than would otherwise have been the case for any given inflation target, if government spending is absorbing a growing share of national output. In the output-gap model of inflation, for example, a 1 per cent excess demand at the level of real GDP can be eliminated only by a 2 per cent contraction in real private demand if the state is spending 50 per cent of GDP and will not cut its own spending.

A similar conclusion can be drawn from the simple quantity theory of money, according to which inflation is the result of too much money chasing too few goods. Here, a switch of output from the private to the public sector is directly inflationary. This is because only the non-socialised part of the economy has a demand for money and increased socialisation reduces the supply of goods that the private sector has available to soak up money balances. This 'share' effect is distinct from the adverse effects of tax-and-spend policies on the level and growth of real GDP considered in the previous paragraph.

Historically, central bankers have frequently expressed concern about the funding pressures caused by budget deficits. Indeed, the huge increase in the national debt during World Wars I and II meant that its management was the dominant consideration in UK monetary policy, for decades afterwards (see Goodhart, 1999, 2003). The hyper-inflations observed during the last century also gave rise to concern that it was impossible to control the price level if the stock of government debt rose too fast for too long.

The logical end-point of this concern is the Fiscal Theory of the Price Level (FTPL), which claims, in its strongest form, that the price level is dominated by the behaviour of the stock of government bonds rather than the nominal money stock. This leaves the central bank with no ability to control inflation. The FTPL is highly controversial, and people who want to know more should read the article by McCallum and Nelson in *Oxford Review of Economic Policy* (2005). Fortunately, the consensus appears to be that the traditional tools of monetary policy remain effective in the face of large budget deficits, even if the output and employment costs of counter-inflationary policies may be exacerbated, leading to political criticism of the central bank.

These issues appear to be well understood by the ECB, which has had to live with the adverse consequences of the Eurozone's high tax and regulatory burdens from the start of European Monetary Union (EMU). Such concerns are starting to enter the policy debate in Britain, and could become a source of tension as the socialisation of the British economy reaches Continental levels.

A specific worry is the extent to which fiscal positions now appear to be hypersensitive to boom–bust cycles in the financial markets, which means that myopic governments have a strong incentive to lean on central banks not to deflate speculative financial bubbles. This issue was examined by Jaeger and Schuknecht (2004). The authors found that conventional estimates of revenue elasticities tended to seriously underestimate the response of tax receipts to output during periods of financial boom and bust.

8   POLICY CONCLUSIONS

This chapter pulls together some of the ideas discussed earlier, analyses how different forms of franchise can affect the levels of tax and spending, and discusses how taxation and representation can be better aligned. It concludes with a call for a more open and mature political debate on these issues.

The political background

British politics appear to have entered an unusually fluid stage at the time of writing, with both the Conservatives and Liberal Democrats having recently changed their leaders and with Mr Blair having promised to stand down within a year. The Conservatives are running ahead of Labour in the opinion polls for the first time in years. In terms of Hayek's Triangle, it is clear that the new Conservative leader, David Cameron, is attempting to move his party's perceived ideological image from the classical-liberal point established under Margaret Thatcher to an interventionist one, and is arguably trying to outflank New Labour on the left. This is a typical paternalist wealth conservator's strategy, and may work at the electoral level, even if one has reservations about the economic implications and whether there is any point in the Conservative Party's further existence if it dare not differentiate its product from Labour's. Mr Cameron's somewhat pusillanimous rebranding operation may have simply misjudged the public mood – there is evidence from an opinion poll carried out by the Taxpayers' Alliance, released on 26 August 2006, that there is a far greater appetite for liberal-market policies than the UK political establishment has realised (see www.taxpayersalliance.com and the *Sunday Times* and *The Business* for 28 August 2006) – but it is readily comprehended using the public choice arguments of Chapter 6. The Conservatives seem to be assuming that government intervention has reached the point where it has become impossible for them to attract sufficient support based on proposals for a smaller state, although this is no more than an untested hypothesis in the absence of a politician brave enough to challenge it. As with all IEA publications, the purpose of this monograph is not to set out the policies that politicians should adopt to get elected but, rather, to set out the economic principles that should underlie policy, based on an examination of the evidence.

Costs of an 'excessive' public sector

The earlier chapters of this monograph reviewed the international literature concerning the harmful effects of 'excessive' – by which is meant higher-than-optimal – public expenditure on economic growth, output and welfare. Government spending as a percentage of GDP has grown dramatically in the last 100 years, and it is possible that output in the UK would be some 95 per cent higher today if spending had been stabilised at its late 1950s levels. All sectors of society, including the very poor, would almost certainly have been better off as a consequence; in part because of the greatly enhanced life opportunities that would have been available to all levels of society in the more dynamic economy that would have resulted.

Limited returns from wars on waste

Higher-than-optimal government spending is wasteful in two senses and becomes increasingly so as the role of the state expands. The first form of waste is that the state destroys utility if the marginal benefit of extra government spending is less than the opportunity cost of the taxes needed to pay for it. The second is that the government does not make effective use of the resources placed at its disposal because of bureaucratic incompetence and political infighting. If UK government spending were as efficient as that in low-spending countries such as Japan, the USA and Australia, current government services could be provided for £40–80 billion less than their current cost. The empirical evidence that waste is an increasing function of the size of the government sector suggests, however, that high levels of government efficiency cannot be attained without lower spending levels than are observed in Europe. Waste is always morally inexcusable and less waste may well follow in the wake of a smaller government sector, but a politically hyped attack on waste is unlikely to be the mechanism by which a smaller government sector is created.

'Bad buys' in the UK tax system

The British tax system is not well designed to achieve economic efficiency, and the situation has deteriorated in recent years to the extent that few private economic agents can estimate their future tax liabilities when engaging in long-lived economic commitments. This uncertainty is a strong disincentive to human and physical capital formation, long-term saving and entrepreneurship. The UK would, however, still have an inefficient way of financing its public spending even if the current tax system were fixed and immutable. In particular, marginal rates are too high and taxes are levied in an opaque fashion.

Regional injustice

Furthermore, there is considerable regional injustice within the UK. Much of south and eastern England is effectively a low-spend economy – but not low-tax – while Scotland, Wales, Northern Ireland and parts of the north have externally funded government spending levels akin to those found in the now defunct communist economies. Large transfers take place from the south of the UK, which is under-represented in parliamentary terms, to the over-represented 'old' north and to the Celtic fringe. It may, at first sight, appear strange that economic growth is slower in the recipient regions of the UK, despite these inflows. The particular way in which regional transfers take place actually means, however, that they give rise to welfare losses among both recipient communities and those areas that are taxed to finance the redistribution.

In summary, the political debate about public spending today is at its most sterile when there is more to be concerned about than at any time since the mid-1970s.

What should be done?

The evidence is that UK government spending needs to be scaled back substantially as a share of GDP, if it is to be brought closer to its social optimum, and there is no welfare-based case for further increases in the spending share, regardless of whether these occur through design or inadequate spending discipline. If it is assumed, as a working hypothesis, that the main factor leading to government spending being pushed beyond the share of national output at which social welfare is maximised is the lack of correlation between taxation and representation, then there are a number of theoretical solutions to this problem. It is most definitely not being claimed that all are desirable or, in some cases, intended to be any more than the thought experiments widely engaged in by theoretical economists in order to test the consequences of their models. The analysis starts with the two most radical, and least realistic, of these thought experiments.

A poll tax?

First, one course would be to fund all state spending using a poll tax, so that there was a direct and complete link between taxation and representation. This eliminates the 'lynch mob' problem entirely and arguably delivers the nearest approach to an optimal perfect-competition outcome when resources are distributed equally. It is clearly not feasible politics, however, nor is it desirable on ability-to-pay grounds. Even so, it is worth noting that a surprisingly large amount of the literature in theoretical economics assumes that public spending is funded out of 'non-distortionary lump-sum taxes', which is simply a euphemism for a poll tax. This needs to be borne in mind when assessing the policy implications drawn from such models. On equity grounds, a poll tax can be justified to finance some government expenditure lines but, in general, it is more reasonable for people to pay for government spending in proportion to their income.

A property qualification to vote?

Another way of closing the gap between representation and taxation would be to weight votes – at least in part – according to the individual's tax contribution, a system that used to be known as a property franchise when most taxes were levied on fixed assets, such as houses. It is an interesting historical phenomenon that where property franchises have existed – for example, in Britain in the eighteenth and nineteenth centuries – rapid economic growth has often resulted, with the result that the right to vote was then progressively spread more widely through the population (Briggs, 1970, contains an interesting account of the mid-nineteenth-century debate on the extension of the franchise, while Walmsley, 2006, considers the links between universal suffrage and economic and social decline in a highly provocative IEA Web Discussion Paper). Barro (1997) also found that increasing democracy beyond a certain point led to slower economic growth, while emphasising that dictatorships were as likely to produce extremely bad economic outcomes as better-than-average ones. This suggests that a rationally risk-averse person would never opt for a dictatorship over a democracy, even on purely economic grounds.

Constitutional reform

The conclusion at this point is that representative democracy remains the least bad form of government available, to paraphrase Winston Churchill, but that its susceptibility to vested interests will always lead to a higher ratio of government spending to national output than is optimal, unless the 'plundering' tendencies of the political class are constrained by constitutionally guaranteed economic, as well as political and civil, rights. This is where the independence, integrity and efficiency of a nation's legal institutions become crucial, as Bastiat realised with brilliant insight one and a half centuries ago (reprinted as Bastiat, 2001).

While the best means that an economic liberal can hope to employ in order to limit the damage done by vested interest groups is to maximise the link between taxation and representation, it is noteworthy that constitutions that embody a strong degree of direct accountability and low-level local autonomy, such as those of the USA or Switzerland, also seem to end up with lower public spending burdens than less accountable top-down systems, such as the French Napoleonic one, where would-be plunderers are less subject to constraint. Laubach (2005) provides a fascinating analysis of the US system, where both the states and, to a lesser extent, local governments have considerable autonomy, while Lockwood (2005) provides an interesting political economy analysis of the benefits from fiscal decentralisation. Such considerations suggest that the tendency of the political process to push the share of government spending beyond its economically optimal level in Europe results from too little direct democracy, not a surfeit of it. Continental Roman law systems may also provide less constraint on overweening governments than the Anglo-Saxon common-law tradition.

The danger that large fiscal authorities lead to undue public sector aggrandisement, and high levels of rent-seeking, and eventually corruption, is particularly relevant to the EU, where democratic accountability is especially weak. The US federal government is also notoriously extravagant, however, and it is possible that populous political units are simply too remote from the individual voter for the normal democratic checks and balances to apply.

Flat taxes

From an economic viewpoint, there is a strong supply-side case for simple, proportionate flat-rate taxes. There is also, however, a strong political-economy case for flat-rate taxes, because they strengthen the perceived link between spending and taxation, limit the free-rider problem, and encourage politicians and electors to behave more responsibly. Such political-economy considerations go against the normal view that flat-rate income taxes should have a substantial zero-rate threshold before the tax applies.

Contributory social insurance

There is also a strong political case for reintroducing the contributory principle to social insurance, which has been broken increasingly from the 1960s onwards by the growing reliance on discretionary benefits (see Lawlor, 1998). Restoring the contributory principle would allow Britain to adopt more liberal arrangements towards economic migrants, who would be entitled to benefits only after they had paid appropriate National Insurance contributions. Contributory social insurance systems allow workers to link the benefits they receive with the cost of those benefits, and should lead to more rational voting behaviour.[1]

---

1   It is also worth noting that contributory systems facilitate 'contracting out' and voluntary forms of privatisation that can be an effective check on the size of welfare benefits.

Vouchers for health and education

A paradoxical consequence of throwing money at the public services, which could ultimately undermine the post-war welfare state, is that it has made a voucher system financially feasible for the first time. Free market economists, and social liberals, have long favoured replacing the state's monopoly supply of services such as health and education with vouchers – because vouchers increase choice, encourage efficiency and empower the poor – but have been previously discouraged by the apparently higher costs. The per capita cost of health and education has now been pushed to the point where it would be possible to replace the existing public provision of health and education services with private health insurance and state funding of school fees. Insurance-based Continental health systems appear to generate better clinical outcomes than Britain's NHS, while the US experience of education vouchers at the state or city level suggests that they are particularly effective for poorer residents of areas with severe social problems. One additional benefit of vouchers is that they demonstrate to citizens precisely how much they are paying through taxes for government-funded services.

Regional justice

The discussion about vouchers and a more localised approach to government links up with the analysis of regional injustice in Chapter 4. If citizens received health and education vouchers, it would immediately become infeasible to spend *more* per head in areas such as Scotland, Wales, etc. Indeed, a debate could ensue about whether the value of the voucher should be positively related to salaries in each region so that vouchers had a *lower* value in low-cost regions. Alternatively, the value of vouchers could be determined at the regional level, as long as the taxation raised to finance them was also raised at the same governmental level. Finally, it is worth noting that it might well be appropriate to vary welfare benefits by region, in order to avoid permanently pricing the less skilled out of employment.

Time for a mature debate

In an ideal world politicians would be honest about the trade-offs facing the electorate and would attempt to educate the population about the adverse long-run implications of excessive public expenditure on the future growth of their living standards. This approach is, of course, the opposite of that adopted by many of the world's politicians, who sometimes seem to try to get as many people as possible dependent on public employment or means-tested benefits, in an attempt to maximise the proportion of the electorate dependent on the state. This 'pork-barrelling' allows government to concentrate the tax burden on a minority of the electorate, in a manner analogous to the behaviour of a textbook discriminatory monopolist, and is consistent with the market-research-led approach to fighting elections. The latter consists of identifying small groups of key voters in the key marginal constituencies, and offering them generous favours, while ignoring the views and interests of the mass of the population who vote in non-marginal seats. It is easy to be gloomy about the long-term health of democracy when all the political parties employ such techniques, especially if the economy starts to buckle under the strain of excessive taxes and regulations, the young and the gifted emigrate to lower-tax jurisdictions, and large numbers of less productive workers find themselves priced out of employment.

We have noted that national income per head might be nearly twice as high as it is today if it were not for the increase in the proportion of national income taken in taxation since the 1960s. Therefore a mature debate about the level of public spending, the forms of taxation used to raise revenue and the political constraints that are necessary to hold public spending closer to optimal levels should take centre stage both within parties and between parties. Sadly, there is little sign of that mature debate beginning.

REFERENCES

Adam, S. and J. Browne (2006), *A Survey of the UK Tax System*, IFS
Briefing Note no. 9, January (www.ifs.org.uk).

Alfonso, A., L. Schuknecht and T. Tanzi (2003), *Public Sector
Efficiency: An International Comparison*, European Central
Bank Working Paper no. 242, July.

Alfonso, A., W. Ebert, L. Schuknecht and M. Thöne (2005),
Quality of Public Finances and Growth, European Central Bank
Working Paper no. 438, February.

Assenmacher-Wesche, K. and S. Gerlach (2006), *Interpreting
Euro Area Inflation at High and Low Frequencies*, Bank for
International Settlements Working Paper no. 195, February
(www.bis.org).

Atkinson, T. (2005), *Atkinson Review of Government Output
and Productivity for the National Accounts: Final Report*,
Basingstoke: Palgrave Macmillan (also www.statistics.gov.
uk/about/methodology_by_theme/atkinson).

Bacon, R. and W. Eltis (1976), *Britain's Economic Problem: Too Few
Producers*, London and Basingstoke: Macmillan Press.

Balcerowicz, L. (2002), *Post Communist Transition: Some Lessons*,
London: Institute for Economic Affairs.

Barro, R. J. (1974), 'Are government bonds net wealth?', *Journal of
Political Economy*, 82(6).

Barro, R. J. (1997), *Determinants of Economic Growth: A Cross Country Empirical Study*, Cambridge, MA: MIT Press.

Bartholomew, J. (2004), *The Welfare State We're In*, London: Politico's/Methuen.

Bastiat, C. F. (2001), *The Law*, London: Institute for Economic Affairs.

Baumol, W. J. (1967), 'The macroeconomics of unbalanced growth', *American Economic Review*, 57, June.

Beaulier, S. and B. Caplan (2002), *Behavioral Economics and Perverse Effects of the Welfare State*, Department of Economics and Center for Study of Public Choice, George Mason University (www.gmu.edu/department/economics/bcaplan/perfinal.doc).

Becsi, Z. (1996), *Do State and Local Taxes Affect Relative State Growth?*, Federal Reserve Bank of Atlanta, Economic Review, March/April.

Bergström, F. and R. Gidehag (2004), *EU Versus USA*, Stockholm: Timbro (www.timbro.com).

Boerner, K. and S. Uebelmesser (2005), *Migration and the Welfare State: The Economic Power of the Non-Voter*, CESIFO Working Paper no. 1517, August (www.cesifo-group.de).

Booth, P. M. (1998), 'The transition from social insecurity', *Economic Affairs*, 18(1): 2–13.

Booth, P. M. (1999), 'The problems with PAYGO pensions', *Journal of Pensions Management*, 4(3): 229–42.

Bosanquet, N. and B. Gibbs (2005), *The IPOD Generation – Insecure, Pressured, Over-Taxed and Debt-Ridden*, Reform, August (www.reform.co.uk).

Botman, D. and K. Honjo (2006), *Options for Fiscal Consolidation in the United Kingdom*, International Monetary Fund Working Paper WP/06/89, Washington, DC, March (www.imf.org).

Botman, D., D. Laxton, D. Muir and A. Romanov (2006), *A New Open Economy Macro Model for Fiscal Policy Evaluation*, International Monetary Fund Working Paper WP/06/45, Washington, DC, February (www.imf.org).

Briggs, A. (1970), *Victorian People*, Harmondsworth: Pelican.

Briotti, M. G. (2005), *Economic Reactions to Public Finance Consolidation: A Survey of the Literature*, European Central Bank Occasional Paper no. 38, October.

Campos, J., N. R. Ericsson and D. F. Hendry (2005), *General-to-specific Modeling: An Overview and Selected Bibliography*, US Federal Reserve International Finance Discussion Paper no. 838, August (www.federalreserve.gov).

Church, K. B., P. R. Mitchell, P. N. Smith and K. F. Wallis (1993), *Comparative Properties of Models of the UK Economy*, National Institute Economic Review, August.

Crafts, N. (2001), *Supply-Side Policy and British Relative Economic Decline*, Paper presented to HM Treasury Growth Seminar, 3 March (www.hm-treasury.gov.uk).

Darwell, R. (2005), *The Reluctant Managers*, Part 1: *Report on Reforming Whitehall*, Reform, December (www.reform.co.uk).

Davies, E. (1998), *Public Spending*, Harmondsworth: Penguin.

De Avila, D. G. and R. Strauch (2003), *Public Finances and Long-Term Growth in Europe, Evidence from a Panel Data Analysis*, European Central Bank Working Paper no. 246, July.

Department for Communities and Local Government (2006), *House Price Index*, June 2006, Press release, 14 August.

Economist (2006), 'Trouble on Welfare Island', *Economist*, 27 May, pp. 49, 50.

Feinstein, C. H. (1972), *National Income Expenditure and Output of the United Kingdom*, Cambridge: Cambridge University Press.

Freeman, R. (2001), *What Does Modern Growth Analysis Say about Government Policy towards Growth?*, Paper presented to HM Treasury Growth Seminar, 3 March (www.hm-treasury.gov. uk).

Fugeman, D. (1999), *An International Comparison of Taxes and Social Security Contributions*, UK National Statistics, Economic Trends, March.

Funke, K. and C. Nickel (2006), *Does Fiscal Policy Matter for the Trade Account? A Panel Cointegration Study*, European Central Bank Working Paper no. 620, May (www.ecb.int).

Giudice, G., A. Turrini and J. in t' Veld (2003), *Can Fiscal Consolidations Be Expansionary in the EU? Ex-post Evidence and Ex-ante Analysis*, European Commission Economic Papers no. 195, December.

Goodhart, C. A. E. (1999), 'Monetary policy and debt management in the United Kingdom', in K. A. Chrystal (ed.), *Some Historical Viewpoints in Government Debt Structure and Monetary Conditions*, London: Bank of England.

Goodhart, C. A. E. (2003), 'Money and monetary policy', in J. Hirst (ed.), *The Challenge of Change: Fifty Years of Business Economics*, London: Society of Business Economists and Profile Books.

Gould, S. J. (1981), *The Mismeasure of Man*, New York: Norton/ London: Pelican (1984, reprinted in Penguin 1992).

Graham, C. (2005), 'The economics of happiness', *World Economics*, 6(3), July–September.

Grainger, H. (2006), *Trade Union Membership 2005*, London: Department of Trade and Industry (www.dti.gov.uk/ publications).

Habermeier, K. with S. Symansky (1995), *United Germany: The First Five Years, Performance and Policy Issues*, ch. 4, 'Fiscal policy and economic growth', International Monetary Fund Occasional Paper no. 125, Washington, DC.

Harrison, R., K. Nikolov, M. Quinn, G. Ramsay, A. Scott and R. Thomas (2005), *The Bank of England Quarterly Model*, London: Bank of England.

Hauptmeier, S., M. Heipertz and L. Schuknecht (2006), *Expenditure Reform in Industrialised Countries: A Case Study Approach*, European Central Bank Working Paper no. 634, May (www.ecb.int).

Hayek, F. A. (1960), 'Why I am not a Conservative', in *The Constitution of Liberty*, Chicago, IL: University of Chicago Press (p/b edn 1978).

Heath, A. (2006a), *Flat Tax: Towards a British Model*, London: Taxpayers' Alliance (www.taxpayersalliance.com).

Heath, A. (2006b), 'Gain or loss? The UK's growing public sector', in A. Heath and D. B. Smith, *At a Price! The True Cost of Public Spending*, London: Politeia.

Heitger, B. (2002), 'The impact of taxation on unemployment in OECD Countries', *Cato Journal*, 22(2).

Henderson, D. (2000), *Anti-Liberalism 2000*, Wincott Lecture, London: Institute for Economic Affairs.

Hicks, S., A. Walling, D. Heap and D. Livesey (2005), *Public Sector Employment Trends 2005*, London: Office for National Statistics, October.

HM Treasury (2006), *Public Expenditure: Statistical Analyses for 2006* (www.official-documents.co.uk).

Jaeger, A. and L. Schuknecht (2004), *Boom–Bust Phases in Asset Prices and Fiscal Policy Behaviour*, International Monetary Fund Working Paper, Washington, DC, March (www.imf.org).

Jones, F. (2006), *The Effects of Taxes and Benefits on Household Income, 2004–2005*, UK National Statistics, Economic Trends, May.

Joumard, I., P. M. Kongsrud, Y.-S. Nam and R. Price (2004), *Enhancing the Effectiveness of Public Spending: Experience in OECD Countries*, OECD Economics Department Working Paper no. 380, 12 February (www.oecd.org).

Kennedy, P. (1989), *The Rise and Fall of the Great Powers*, London: Fontana Press.

Laubach, T. (2003), *New Evidence on the Interest Rate Effects of Budget Deficits and Debt*, US Federal Reserve Financial and Economics Discussion series no. 2003-12, May.

Laubach, T. (2005), *Fiscal Relations across Levels of Government in the United States*, OECD Economics Department Working Paper no. 462, November (www.oecd.org).

Lawlor, S. (1998), *Beveridge or Brown? Contribution and Redistribution: The Real Social Security Debate*, London: Politeia.

Leach, G. (2003), *The Negative Impact of Taxation on Economic Growth*, London: Reform, September (www.reform.co.uk).

Leiner-Killinger, N., C. Madaschi and M. Ward-Warmedinger (2005), *Trends and Patterns in Working Time across Euro Area Countries 1970–2004: Causes and Consequences*, European Central Bank Occasional Paper no. 41, December (www.ecb.int).

Lightfoot, W. (2005), *For Better, or for Worse? The Economic Record of the Labour Government*, London: Politeia.

Littlewood, J. (2004) *The Stock Market under Labour: For New Labour Read Old*, London: Centre for Policy Studies.

Lockwood, B. (2005), *Fiscal Decentralisation: A Political Economy Perspective*, Warwick Economic Research Papers no. 721, January (www.warwick.ac.uk/fac/soc/economics).

Lomborg, B. (2003), *The Skeptical Environmentalist: Measuring the Real State of the World*, Cambridge: Cambridge University Press.

Looney, A. (2005), *The Effects of Welfare Reform and Related Policies on Single Mothers' Welfare Use and Employment in the 1990s*, US Federal Reserve Board Working Paper 2005-45, January.

MacGrattan, E. (1994), 'The macroeconomic effects of distortionary taxation', *Journal of Monetary Economics*, 33.

MacSearraigh, E., J. Marais and S. Schuster (2006), *Regional Household Income*, UK National Statistics, Economic Trends, August.

Major, J. (2003), *The Erosion of Parliamentary Democracy*, London: Centre for Policy Studies (www.cps.org.uk).

Marais, J. (2006), *Regional Gross Value Added*, UK Office for National Statistics, Economic Trends, February.

Matthews, K., J. Shepherd and V. Sivarajasingham (2006), *Violence Related Injury and the Price of Beer in England and Wales*, Cardiff Economics Working Papers no. E2006/3, January (www.cardiff.ac.uk/carbs/econ/workingpapers).

Mendoza, E. G., A. Razin and L. L. Tesar (1993), *An International Comparison of Tax Systems in Industrial Countries*,

International Monetary Fund Staff Studies, Washington, DC, December.

Meyer, L. H. (2001), *Does Money Matter? The 2001 Homer Jones Memorial Lecture*, Washington University, St Louis, MI, 28 March (US Federal Reserve website, www.federalreserve.gov).

Miles, D., G. Myles and I. Preston (eds) (2002), *The Economics of Public Spending*, Oxford: Oxford University Press.

Minford, P. (2006), *An Agenda for Tax Reform*, London: Centre for Policy Studies (www.cps.org.uk).

Minford, P. and J. Wang (2006), *Public Spending and Growth* (unpublished but downloadable from www.cf.ac.uk/carbs/econ/webbbd/pm.html).

Mueller, D. (2003), *Public Choice III*, Cambridge: Cambridge University Press.

Mullally, L. and N. O'Brien (2006), *Beyond the European Social Model*, London: Open Europe (downloadable from www.openeurope.org.uk; hard copies can be ordered from amy@openeurope.org.uk).

New, D. and D. Hastings (2006), *Regional Economic Indicators*, UK National Statistics, Economic Trends, August.

OECD (Organisation for Economic Cooperation and Development) (1985), *The Role of the Public Sector: Causes and Consequences of the Growth of Government*, OECD Economic Studies, special issue, spring 1985, Paris: OECD.

OECD (1994), *The OECD Jobs Study: Evidence and Explanations*, 2 vols, Paris: OECD, Paris.

OECD (2003), *The Sources of Economic Growth in OECD Countries*, Paris: OECD.

OECD (2006), *OECD Economic Outlook: June 2006*, Paris: OECD.

Office for National Statistics (2002), *ONS Announces Decision on Tax Credit Treatment*, ONS first release, 20 February.

Office for National Statistics (2006a), *Work and Worklessness among Households*, ONS first release, 25 January.

Office for National Statistics (2006b), *Productivity: 1st Quarter 2006*, ONS first release, 3 July.

Office for National Statistics (2006c*)*, *Labour Disputes – New Public–Private Sector Split*, ONS first release, 5 June.

Office for National Statistics (2006d*)*, *Labour Market Statistics: August 2006*, ONS first release, 16 August.

Oxford Review of Economic Policy (1997), 'Business cycles', *Oxford Review of Economic Policy*, 13(3).

Oxford Review of Economic Policy (2005), 'Fiscal policy', *Oxford Review of Economic Policy*, 21(4).

Peacock, A. T. and J. Wiseman (1961), *The Growth of Public Expenditures in the United Kingdom*, London: Oxford University Press.

Philpotts, G. and P. Causer (eds) (2006), *Regional Trends: No. 39: 2006 Edition*, London: Office for National Statistics (www.statistics.gov.uk).

Prescott, E. C. (2004), 'Why do Americans work so much more than Europeans?', *Federal Reserve Bank of Minneapolis Quarterly Review*, 28(1).

Pritchard, A. (2002), *Measuring Productivity Change in the Provision of Public Services*, ONS Economic Trends, May.

Ramsey, F. (1927), 'A contribution to the theory of taxation', *Economic Journal*.

Roberts, P. C. (1989), 'Supply-side economics: an assessment of the American experience in the 1980s', *National Westminster Bank Quarterly Review*, February.

Royal Statistical Society (2003), *Performance Indicators: Good, Bad and Ugly*, 23 October.

Samuelson, P. (1954), 'The pure theory of public expenditures', *Review of Economics and Statistics*, 36(4): 350–56.

Schuknecht, L. and V. Tanzi (2005a), *Reforming Public Expenditure in Industrialised Countries: Are There Trade-Offs?*, European Central Bank Working Paper no. 435, February (www.ecb.int).

Schuknecht, L. and V. Tanzi (2005b), *Reforming Public Spending: Great Gain, Little Pain*, London: Politeia.

Shaw, J. and L. Sibieta (2005), *A Survey of the UK Benefit System*, IFS Briefing Note no. 13, November (www.ifs.org.uk).

Smith, D. B. (1975), 'Public consumption and economic performance', *National Westminster Bank Quarterly Review*, November.

Smith, D. B. (1981), 'The public expenditure debate', *London Business School Economic Outlook*, June.

Smith, D. B. (1998), *Does Increased Public Spending Destroy Jobs and, If So, How Many?*, London: Williams de Broë.

Smith, D. B. (2001), *Public Rags or Private Riches? High Public Spending Makes Us Poor*, London: Politeia.

Smith, D. B. (2002), 'When is Britain's tax-freedom day?', *Economic Affairs*, December.

Smith, D. B. (2005), *Does Britain Have Regional Justice, or Injustice, in Its Public Spending and Taxation?*, London: Williams de Broë.

Smith, D. B. (2006), 'Does Britain have optimal monetary arrangements, and, if not, does it matter?', in P. Booth and K. Matthews (eds), *Issues in Monetary Policy*, London: Edward Elgar.

Snowden, B. (2004), 'The influence of political distortions on economic performance: the contributions of Alberto Alesina', *World Economics*, 5(4).

Snowden, B. (2006), 'The enduring elixir of economic growth: Xavier Sala-i-Martin on the wealth and poverty of nations', *World Economics*, 7(1).

Tanzi, V. (1997), *The Changing Role of the State in the Economy: A Historical Perspective*, International Monetary Fund Working Paper WP/97/114, Washington, DC.

Tanzi, V. (2000), *The Role of the State and the Quality of the Public Sector*, International Monetary Fund Working Paper WP/00/36, Washington, DC.

Tanzi, V. (2004), *A Lower Tax Future? The Economic Role of the State in the 21st Century*, London: Politeia.

Tanzi, V. and L. Schuknecht (1995), *The Growth of Government and the Reform of the State in Industrial Countries*, International Monetary Fund Working Paper WP/95/130, Washington, DC.

Tanzi, V. and L. Schuknecht (2000), *Public Spending in the 20th Century: A Global Perspective*, Cambridge: Cambridge University Press.

Tullock, G., A. Seldon and G. L. Brady (2000), *Government: Whose Obedient Servant? A Primer in Public Choice*, London: Institute for Economic Affairs.

UK Centre for the Measurement of Government Activity (2005), *Improvements in the Methodology for Measuring Government Output*, UK National Statistics, Economic Trends, September.

UK Centre for the Measurement of Government Activity (2006a), *Public Service Productivity: Education*, UK National Statistics, Economic Trends, January.

UK Centre for the Measurement of Government Activity (2006b), *Public Service Productivity: Health*, UK National Statistics, Economic Trends, March.

Walmsley, B. (2006), *The Corruption of Universal Suffrage: Tax, Consent and the Tyranny of the Majority*, Institute for Economic Affairs Web Discussion Paper no. 12, 2 June (www.iea.org.uk).

Warburton, P. (2002), *IEA Yearbook of Government Performance 2002–03*, London: Institute for Economic Affairs.

Wingfield, D., D. Fenwick and K. Smith (2005), *Relative Regional Consumer Price Levels in 2004*, UK National Statistics, Economic Trends, February.

ABOUT THE IEA

The Institute is a research and educational charity (No. CC 235 351), limited by guarantee. Its mission is to improve understanding of the fundamental institutions of a free society by analysing and expounding the role of markets in solving economic and social problems.

The IEA achieves its mission by:

- a high-quality publishing programme
- conferences, seminars, lectures and other events
- outreach to school and college students
- brokering media introductions and appearances

The IEA, which was established in 1955 by the late Sir Antony Fisher, is an educational charity, not a political organisation. It is independent of any political party or group and does not carry on activities intended to affect support for any political party or candidate in any election or referendum, or at any other time. It is financed by sales of publications, conference fees and voluntary donations.

In addition to its main series of publications the IEA also publishes a quarterly journal, *Economic Affairs*.

The IEA is aided in its work by a distinguished international Academic Advisory Council and an eminent panel of Honorary Fellows. Together with other academics, they review prospective IEA publications, their comments being passed on anonymously to authors. All IEA papers are therefore subject to the same rigorous independent refereeing process as used by leading academic journals.

IEA publications enjoy widespread classroom use and course adoptions in schools and universities. They are also sold throughout the world and often translated/reprinted.

Since 1974 the IEA has helped to create a world-wide network of 100 similar institutions in over 70 countries. They are all independent but share the IEA's mission.

Views expressed in the IEA's publications are those of the authors, not those of the Institute (which has no corporate view), its Managing Trustees, Academic Advisory Council members or senior staff.

Members of the Institute's Academic Advisory Council, Honorary Fellows, Trustees and Staff are listed on the following page.

The Institute gratefully acknowledges financial support for its publications programme and other work from a generous benefaction by the late Alec and Beryl Warren.

The Institute of Economic Affairs
2 Lord North Street, Westminster, London SW1P 3LB
Tel: 020 7799 8900
Fax: 020 7799 2137
Email: iea@iea.org.uk
Internet: iea.org.uk

Director General	John Blundell

Editorial Director	Professor Philip Booth

Managing Trustees

Chairman: Professor D R Myddelton

Kevin Bell	Professor Patrick Minford
Robert Boyd	Professor Martin Ricketts
Michael Fisher	Professor J R Shackleton
Michael Hintze	Sir Peter Walters
Malcolm McAlpine	Linda Whetstone

Academic Advisory Council

Chairman: Professor Martin Ricketts

Graham Bannock	Professor Stephen C Littlechild
Professor Norman Barry	Dr Eileen Marshall
Dr Roger Bate	Professor Antonio Martino
Professor Donald J Boudreaux	Dr Anja Merz
Professor John Burton	Julian Morris
Professor Forrest Capie	Paul Ormerod
Professor Steven N S Cheung	Professor David Parker
Professor Tim Congdon	Dr Mark Pennington
Professor N F R Crafts	Professor Victoria Curzon Price
Professor David de Meza	Professor Colin Robinson
Professor Kevin Dowd	Professor Charles K Rowley
Professor Richard A Epstein	Professor Pascal Salin
Nigel Essex	Dr Razeen Sally
Professor David Greenaway	Professor Pedro Schwartz
Dr Ingrid A Gregg	Jane S Shaw
Walter E Grinder	Professor W Stanley Siebert
Professor Steve H Hanke	Dr Elaine Sternberg
Professor Keith Hartley	Professor James Tooley
Professor David Henderson	Professor Nicola Tynan
Professor Peter M Jackson	Professor Roland Vaubel
Dr Jerry Jordan	Professor Lawrence H White
Dr Lynne Kiesling	Professor Walter E Williams
Professor Daniel B Klein	Professor Geoffrey E Wood

Honorary Fellows

Professor Armen A Alchian	Professor Chiaki Nishiyama
Professor Michael Beenstock	Professor Sir Alan Peacock
Sir Samuel Brittan	Professor Ben Roberts
Professor James M Buchanan	Professor Anna J Schwartz
Professor Ronald H Coase	Professor Vernon L Smith
Dr R M Hartwell	Professor Gordon Tullock
Professor Terence W Hutchison	Professor Sir Alan Walters
Professor David Laidler	Professor Basil S Yamey
Professor Dennis S Lees	

Other papers recently published by the IEA include:

WHO, What and Why?
Transnational Government, Legitimacy and the World Health Organization
Roger Scruton
Occasional Paper 113; ISBN 0 255 36487 3; £8.00

The World Turned Rightside Up
A New Trading Agenda for the Age of Globalisation
John C. Hulsman
Occasional Paper 114; ISBN 0 255 36495 4; £8.00

The Representation of Business in English Literature
Introduced and edited by Arthur Pollard
Readings 53; ISBN 0 255 36491 1; £12.00

Anti-Liberalism 2000
The Rise of New Millennium Collectivism
David Henderson
Occasional Paper 115; ISBN 0 255 36497 0; £7.50

Capitalism, Morality and Markets
Brian Griffiths, Robert A. Sirico, Norman Barry & Frank Field
Readings 54; ISBN 0 255 36496 2; £7.50

A Conversation with Harris and Seldon
Ralph Harris & Arthur Seldon
Occasional Paper 116; ISBN 0 255 36498 9; £7.50

Malaria and the DDT Story
Richard Tren & Roger Bate
Occasional Paper 117; ISBN 0 255 36499 7; £10.00

A Plea to Economists Who Favour Liberty: Assist the Everyman
Daniel B. Klein
Occasional Paper 118; ISBN 0 255 36501 2; £10.00

The Changing Fortunes of Economic Liberalism
Yesterday, Today and Tomorrow
David Henderson
Occasional Paper 105 (new edition); ISBN 0 255 36520 9; £12.50

The Global Education Industry
Lessons from Private Education in Developing Countries
James Tooley
Hobart Paper 141 (new edition); ISBN 0 255 36503 9; £12.50

Saving Our Streams
The Role of the Anglers' Conservation Association in
Protecting English and Welsh Rivers
Roger Bate
Research Monograph 53; ISBN 0 255 36494 6; £10.00

Better Off Out?
The Benefits or Costs of EU Membership
Brian Hindley & Martin Howe
Occasional Paper 99 (new edition); ISBN 0 255 36502 0; £10.00

Buckingham at 25
Freeing the Universities from State Control
Edited by James Tooley
Readings 55; ISBN 0 255 36512 8; £15.00

Lectures on Regulatory and Competition Policy
Irwin M. Stelzer
Occasional Paper 120; ISBN 0 255 36511 X; £12.50

Misguided Virtue
False Notions of Corporate Social Responsibility
David Henderson
Hobart Paper 142; ISBN 0 255 36510 1; £12.50

HIV and Aids in Schools
The Political Economy of Pressure Groups and Miseducation
Barrie Craven, Pauline Dixon, Gordon Stewart & James Tooley
Occasional Paper 121; ISBN 0 255 36522 5; £10.00

The Road to Serfdom
The Reader's Digest *condensed version*
Friedrich A. Hayek
Occasional Paper 122; ISBN 0 255 36530 6; £7.50

Bastiat's *The Law*
Introduction by Norman Barry
Occasional Paper 123; ISBN 0 255 36509 8; £7.50

A Globalist Manifesto for Public Policy
Charles Calomiris
Occasional Paper 124; ISBN 0 255 36525 x; £7.50

Euthanasia for Death Duties
Putting Inheritance Tax Out of Its Misery
Barry Bracewell-Milnes
Research Monograph 54; ISBN 0 255 36513 6; £10.00

Liberating the Land
The Case for Private Land-use Planning
Mark Pennington
Hobart Paper 143; ISBN 0 255 36508 x; £10.00

IEA Yearbook of Government Performance 2002/2003
Edited by Peter Warburton
Yearbook 1; ISBN 0 255 36532 2; £15.00

Britain's Relative Economic Performance, 1870–1999
Nicholas Crafts
Research Monograph 55; ISBN 0 255 36524 1; £10.00

Should We Have Faith in Central Banks?
Otmar Issing
Occasional Paper 125; ISBN 0 255 36528 4; £7.50

The Dilemma of Democracy
Arthur Seldon
Hobart Paper 136 (reissue); ISBN 0 255 36536 5; £10.00

Capital Controls: a 'Cure' Worse Than the Problem?
Forrest Capie
Research Monograph 56; ISBN 0 255 36506 3; £10.00

The Poverty of 'Development Economics'
Deepak Lal
Hobart Paper 144 (reissue); ISBN 0 255 36519 5; £15.00

Should Britain Join the Euro?
The Chancellor's Five Tests Examined
Patrick Minford
Occasional Paper 126; ISBN 0 255 36527 6; £7.50

Post-Communist Transition: Some Lessons
Leszek Balcerowicz
Occasional Paper 127; ISBN 0 255 36533 0; £7.50

A Tribute to Peter Bauer
John Blundell et al.
Occasional Paper 128; ISBN 0 255 36531 4; £10.00

Employment Tribunals
Their Growth and the Case for Radical Reform
J. R. Shackleton
Hobart Paper 145; ISBN 0 255 36515 2; £10.00

Fifty Economic Fallacies Exposed
Geoffrey E. Wood
Occasional Paper 129; ISBN 0 255 36518 7; £12.50

A Market in Airport Slots

Keith Boyfield (editor), David Starkie, Tom Bass & Barry Humphreys
Readings 56; ISBN 0 255 36505 5; £10.00

Money, Inflation and the Constitutional Position of the Central Bank

Milton Friedman & Charles A. E. Goodhart
Readings 57; ISBN 0 255 36538 1; £10.00

railway.com

Parallels between the Early British Railways and the ICT Revolution
Robert C. B. Miller
Research Monograph 57; ISBN 0 255 36534 9; £12.50

The Regulation of Financial Markets

Edited by Philip Booth & David Currie
Readings 58; ISBN 0 255 36551 9; £12.50

Climate Alarmism Reconsidered

Robert L. Bradley Jr
Hobart Paper 146; ISBN 0 255 36541 1; £12.50

Government Failure: E. G. West on Education

Edited by James Tooley & James Stanfield
Occasional Paper 130; ISBN 0 255 36552 7; £12.50

Waging the War of Ideas

John Blundell
Second edition
Occasional Paper 131; ISBN 0 255 36547 0; £12.50

Corporate Governance: Accountability in the Marketplace

Elaine Sternberg
Second edition
Hobart Paper 147; ISBN 0 255 36542 x; £12.50

The Land Use Planning System
Evaluating Options for Reform
John Corkindale
Hobart Paper 148; ISBN 0 255 36550 0; £10.00

Economy and Virtue
Essays on the Theme of Markets and Morality
Edited by Dennis O'Keeffe
Readings 59; ISBN 0 255 36504 7; £12.50

Free Markets Under Siege
Cartels, Politics and Social Welfare
Richard A. Epstein
Occasional Paper 132; ISBN 0 255 36553 5; £10.00

Unshackling Accountants
D. R. Myddelton
Hobart Paper 149; ISBN 0 255 36559 4; £12.50

The Euro as Politics
Pedro Schwartz
Research Monograph 58; ISBN 0 255 36535 7; £12.50

Pricing Our Roads
Vision and Reality
Stephen Glaister & Daniel J. Graham
Research Monograph 59; ISBN 0 255 36562 4; £10.00

The Role of Business in the Modern World
Progress, Pressures, and Prospects for the Market Economy
David Henderson
Hobart Paper 150; ISBN 0 255 36548 9; £12.50

Public Service Broadcasting Without the BBC?
Alan Peacock
Occasional Paper 133; ISBN 0 255 36565 9; £10.00

The ECB and the Euro: the First Five Years
Otmar Issing
Occasional Paper 134; ISBN 0 255 36555 1; £10.00

Towards a Liberal Utopia?
Edited by Philip Booth
Hobart Paperback 32; ISBN 0 255 36563 2; £15.00

The Way Out of the Pensions Quagmire
Philip Booth & Deborah Cooper
Research Monograph 60; ISBN 0 255 36517 9; £12.50

Black Wednesday
A Re-examination of Britain's Experience in the Exchange Rate Mechanism
Alan Budd
Occasional Paper 135; ISBN 0 255 36566 7; £7.50

Crime: Economic Incentives and Social Networks
Paul Ormerod
Hobart Paper 151; ISBN 0 255 36554 3; £10.00

The Road to Serfdom *with* **The Intellectuals and Socialism**
Friedrich A. Hayek
Occasional Paper 136; ISBN 0 255 36576 4; £10.00

Money and Asset Prices in Boom and Bust
Tim Congdon
Hobart Paper 152; ISBN 0 255 36570 5; £10.00

The Dangers of Bus Re-regulation
and Other Perspectives on Markets in Transport
John Hibbs et al.
Occasional Paper 137; ISBN 0 255 36572 1; £10.00

The New Rural Economy
Change, Dynamism and Government Policy
Berkeley Hill et al.
Occasional Paper 138; ISBN 0 255 36546 2; £15.00

The Benefits of Tax Competition
Richard Teather
Hobart Paper 153; ISBN 0 255 36569 1; £12.50

Wheels of Fortune
Self-funding Infrastructure and the Free Market Case for a Land Tax
Fred Harrison
Hobart Paper 154; ISBN 0 255 36589 6; £12.50

Were 364 Economists All Wrong?
Edited by Philip Booth
Readings 60
ISBN-10: 0 255 36588 8; ISBN-13: 978 0 255 36588 8; £10.00

Europe After the 'No' Votes
Mapping a New Economic Path
Patrick A. Messerlin
Occasional Paper 139
ISBN-10: 0 255 36580 2; ISBN-13: 978 0 255 36580 2; £10.00

The Railways, the Market and the Government
John Hibbs et al.
Readings 61
ISBN-10: 0 255 36567 5; ISBN-13: 978 0 255 36567 3; £12.50

Corruption: The World's Big C
Cases, Causes, Consequences, Cures
Ian Senior
Research Monograph 61
ISBN-10: 0 255 36571 3; ISBN-13: 978 0 255 36571 0; £12.50

Sir Humphrey's Legacy
Facing Up to the Cost of Public Sector Pensions
Neil Record
Hobart Paper 156
ISBN-10: 0 255 36578 0; ISBN-13: 978 0 255 36578 9; £10.00

The Economics of Law
Cento Veljanovski
Second edition
Hobart Paper 157
ISBN-10: 0 255 36561 6; ISBN-13: 978 0 255 36561 1; £12.50

To order copies of currently available IEA papers, or to enquire about availability, please contact:

Gazelle
IEA orders
FREEPOST RLYS-EAHU-YSCZ
White Cross Mills
Hightown
Lancaster LA1 4XS

Tel: 01524 68765
Fax: 01524 63232
Email: sales@gazellebooks.co.uk

The IEA also offers a subscription service to its publications. For a single annual payment, currently £40.00 in the UK, you will receive every monograph the IEA publishes during the course of a year and discounts on our extensive back catalogue. For more information, please contact:

Adam Myers
Subscriptions
The Institute of Economic Affairs
2 Lord North Street
London SW1P 3LB

Tel: 020 7799 8920
Fax: 020 7799 2137
Website: www.iea.org.uk